40 YEARS 40,000 SALES CALLS

Thoughts on Radio and Advertising Based on a Lifetime of Customer Contact

BARRY DRAKE

Copyright © 2014 Barry Drake
All rights reserved.

ISBN: 1503099318
ISBN 13: 9781503099319

About the Author

Barry Drake is best known as a "radio guy," although he served as CEO of a sixty-two-station television group as well. He has been on the programming and production side of the radio business, sold locally in markets large and small, sold nationally, and managed radio stations in all formats, sizes, and market conditions.

In 1984, Drake joined Keymarket Communications as general manager, first in Baton Rouge and then in Houston, before being named president of the group in 1988. Keymarket was sold to River City Broadcasting in 1995, and in 1996, River City was purchased by Sinclair Broadcast Group, where Drake was named CEO of radio and then CEO of television in 1999.

He is no stranger to the finance side of the industry, having years of experience working with equity sponsors, the public market, and lenders to structure companies and deals.

In 2002, Drake formed Backyard Broadcasting with private equity sponsor Boston Ventures. The group grew to thirty radio stations in six markets, then was sold in 2013.

During his career, Drake stayed close to the action by committing himself to making sales calls, some with sales people, others on his own. He has called on a wide range of businesses: chains with billions of dollars in volume and small, single-location retailers grossing less than $1 million annually.

What Barry Drake enjoys most is listening to business owners talk about advertising and what works.

DEDICATION

To Miles
May your generation know a world of peace, love, and joy.

TABLE OF CONTENTS

Introduction

The story you are about to read is true, at least to the best of my memory. I realize others may recall the facts surrounding the events described differently. The opinions expressed are mine, the outcome of what I learned over forty years while making forty thousand sales calls.

The forty years dates back to June 4, 1973, my first day as a full-time radio station employee. The forty thousand calls varied greatly over the forty years. Calls include those I made as a local salesman, a national rep, a manager, group head, and a few when I was a program director/air personality and would accompany sales people to see our advertisers.

As a national rep, I naturally did business for stations all across the United States. As far as actually calling on customers and conducting business, I count thirty-two states and the District of Columbia. Market size ranged from New York City to Ponchatoula, Louisiana.

Customers seen include anyone from the owner of a small frame shop to the president of a department store chain. There were dozens of auto dealers. On the advertising agency side, calls include those made on agency principals, as well as junior media buyers.

In some cases, I use real names; however, I have omitted or changed some names— where appropriate, and where I've simply forgotten the details.

Much of the story flows chronologically. Part one deals with my background and growing up. I include this to give the reader a sense of why I think the way I do. During the story, I call "time out" six times for special reports.

Part six is an account of where radio is today, and at the conclusion, based on the experiences of forty thousand sales calls, I attempt to offer some thoughts on what may be coming in the near future and a few prescriptions for moving forward. Feel free to agree or disagree. Readers compelled to comment may reach me by email: barrydrake4040@gmail.com.

This book was written primarily during the period of December 2013 through March 2014. I am not responsible for any changes in the world order after that time.

One hundred percent of the net proceeds from the sale of this book will be donated to the Broadcasters Foundation of America, a charity devoted to providing financial assistance to radio and television broadcasters in acute need. The Broadcasters Foundation does not endorse or subscribe to the views expressed herein.

Barry Drake
April 1, 2014

PART ONE
THE REALLY OLD DAYS

CHAPTER 1

SIGNING ON

As Lady Gaga sings, "I was born this way." When I came along in 1951, my mother and father, Ann and Ron Drake, were working for WHP radio in Harrisburg, Pennsylvania. My father was the morning and evening announcer, working what was called a "split shift," and my mother was the copywriter.

Ann was already working at WHP when Ron was hired. After graduating from high school, she worked for a year at the telephone company and lived at home to save up some money. Then she went off to Marjorie Webster Junior College in Washington, DC, to get her degree in creative writing. Ann's dream was to write drama for radio. This was 1944.

After graduation, Ann came back to Harrisburg and got an appointment with Abe Redmond, the general manager of WHP. Abe, and his brother, Dick, sold all the local commercial time on the station. At that time, most of the programming came from the network, and there were only a couple of minutes each hour for the local stations to sell, similar to today's television prime time model. Abe's wife, Bea, was the office manager.

Ann showed up and pitched Mr. Redmond on her writing skills and her desire to create shows. Abe Redmond responded, "Young lady, we do shows here. They are sixty seconds in length. You're hired."

Abe and Dick were now free to spend time selling new customers because Ann would do the follow-up work and write all the commercials. Every day she would go out to see the shopkeepers and the bankers and the grocers who had purchased time, question them on what they wanted to accomplish, and create copy to bring the advertisers sales results.

When a year had passed, Ann was eligible for a vacation. After a week away, she returned to the station and detected a buzz in the hallways. Bea, Abe's wife, pulled her aside and said, "Ann, while you were gone, a new, young announcer started. And wait till you see him." A few minutes later, Ann walked into the room adjoining the announcer booth where Ron Drake was working. He turned, their eyes met, and it was love at first sight.

Two years later Ron and Ann were married, and two years after that I came along. At this point, Ann decided to leave the station and become a full-time mother to me and, over the next few years, my two brothers.

My father continued to work for the station and remained at WHP until his retirement in August of 1982, a thirty-five-year run fueled by the spirit of the times: a baby boom, a dynamic American economy, a changing media landscape, the fun and excitement of rock 'n' roll, and—yes, of course—great ratings.

CHAPTER 2

RADIO WITH PICTURES

Dad's first big opportunity came along with the sign-on of WHP television in 1953. CBS, and the now-defunct Dumont Network, supplied a few hours of programming every day. There was no local news yet, but after about a year, the station created its first locally produced television program, *TV Teen Time*. It was a local talent show starring kids, mostly teenagers, along the same format as the nationally telecast *Ted Mack Amateur Hour.* Viewers today would find it similar to *American Idol* with auditions held for weeks on site at the station offices before the show began to air. The announcer would begin the festivities, "Welcome to *TV Teen Time*, and here is your host, Ron Drake."

Doing *TV Teen Time* in the afternoon, Dad continued on the radio at night. The network radio shows were now moving to television, leaving the radio station with hours to program. So, on the radio show, Ron Drake had time to play music, interject commentary, warmth, and humor and was able to cross promote *TV Teen Time* and its talent.

By 1956, music was changing. Without asking permission or advice, Dad began to slip in songs from Elvis, The Everly Brothers, Bill Haley, and Connie Francis. Suddenly, Ron Drake was doing record hops and hosting live rock 'n' roll shows on the weekends.

Meanwhile, WHP's management was taking notice of a local TV show just 100 miles down the road, *Philadelphia Bandstand* with Dick Clark. This was the original show that ran for two hours daily on WFIL-TV, Philadelphia, PA. It went on to become *American Bandstand* and moved to Hollywood on the ABC network.

WHP-TV management was beginning to find *TV Teen Time*, and the work involved to root out worthy talent, to be tiresome. What better way to fill up local programming hours than by playing records and just letting some high school kids come in and dance? And there was already a credible host in-house, Ron Drake.

Ron Drake's Record Room took to the air in 1957 and was a big hit with viewers.

There was no programming staff, and the production crew was a holdover from *TV Teen Time*. Dad had to direct it all himself. He gave up the radio show to devote his time exclusively to *Record Room*. Mom's job was to sit in our living room at home and watch Dick Clark every day, writing down each of the songs he played. I was in first grade by this time, so, when I got home from school, I could write well enough to keep track of the songs if Mom had to go make dinner or take care of my brother.

There was constant commotion during the *Record Room* years. The producing and hosting of a daily television show, and live appearances and shows every weekend, kept Dad on the run. Even the relatively peaceful Sunday afternoon was regularly invaded with unexpected visits from the high schoolers who danced on the show. They'd show up at our house and ask to see Dad and just hang out for a while.

We got many crank calls at home. One night was awful. Someone called while Dad was out doing a record hop. The caller identified himself as a state policeman and told Mom that Dad was attacked after the hop by a gang of rowdies who left him in such bad shape he had to be taken to the hospital. The caller said he would get back to us as soon as he had more information and then hung up. No follow-up call ever came. It was very scary, until about thirty minutes later when Dad walked through the front door just fine. It was a prank. We had our phone number changed and unlisted, but it didn't help. Too many people always had the number or could get it from someone. We had our home number changed so many times during those years I had a hard time keeping it straight.

When I started third grade and had to fill out a registration form on the first day of school, I just left the space for home phone blank.

Eventually *Record Room* was cancelled due to complaints from the neighbors. WHP was in a downtown Harrisburg office building, and a hundred or so teenagers storming in and disrupting business every afternoon just got to be too much. No one wanted to go to the trouble or the expense to move the station or the show to another site, so it was the end.

At the same time *Record Room* was winding down, Abe Redmond died suddenly. Just like that, there was no TV show and my parents' mentor and professional father figure was gone.

As soon as new management arrived, the entire atmosphere at WHP became more business-like, more corporate. The engineers and announcers became unionized, and many of the people I used to see when I visited the stations with my Dad were no longer around.

Management decided my father would return to radio. He was put in afternoon drive, 2:00 to 6:00 p.m. The music playlist was toned way down. The new general manager preferred Perry Como to Chuck Berry. Things got very quiet for a while, but that turned out to be temporary. The wildest days were yet to come.

CHAPTER 3

READY FOR PRIME TIME

B y the end of 1959, management felt a need to make a move with WHP-AM. The station was the main source of the company's revenue and all of the profit. Television was still young and FM not yet a factor. What the company sought for WHP-AM were bigger ratings and higher advertising rates in radio's prime time, morning drive. Instead of conducting a search for out-of-market talent, the station turned to what it deemed to be its second most valuable asset, (the first being its superior technical facility of 5,000 watts at 580AM), the afternoon host, Ron Drake. This was more appealing to management from an efficiency standpoint. Bringing in someone from the outside meant higher costs and the risk of the unknown.

The good news for all involved was the idea worked. Even before the first show aired, much talk circulated about Ron Drake's move to mornings. An advertising campaign ran on Channel 21 to promote the show, and print ads were placed, as well, in the *Harrisburg Patriot News*.

The show was loaded with features; CBS network news, the local news, and the national weather service report from the airport took up almost twenty minutes of each half hour. From the experience Dad had during those days when the network programs were being replaced by local news and music, he was able to run these features and interject the warmth, humor, and flavor of a personality who was linked to the local market.

The new morning show was an instant hit, but it had really been in the works for thirteen years. For Harrisburg listeners to wake up with Ron Drake was more natural than watching the sun come up over Blue Mountain and the Susquehanna River. After all, Central Pennsylvanians had been hearing his voice, watching him on television, and seeing him in the community since 1947. Ron Drake did such a good job of immersing himself in the area that although he was a native of New York City, it became widely accepted that he was born and raised in Central Pennsylvania.

As the morning ratings on WHP continued to soar, it was inevitable they would be noticed by radio operators around the country looking to improve their own stations. Offers to move to other markets presented themselves; Cincinnati and San Diego were two that stood out. My father politely refused. He understood better than anyone did what was going on and maintained a very realistic view of the situation.

Dad used to tell me, because he knew the market so well and had such great rapport with the audience, what he did on the air at WHP may or may not work in any other city. Dad also liked the freedom. "Look," he'd say, "here I can do anything I want to on the air and I don't have to worry about any rules the manager or some research consultant cooked up."

Dad certainly did love the job. In all the years I lived at home, not once did I ever hear him voice any complaint about having to go to work. If anything, it was the opposite. The threat of snow? Dad was on his way into the studios, usually in time to make a guest appearance on the 11:00 p.m. television news to prepare the audience for the next morning. Election night? On duty. The night during the Cuban missile crisis when the Soviets shot down our U-2 plane? Into the stations in case there was a war. During Hurricane Agnes, Dad stayed on the air for several days throughout the flooding with emergency bulletins, instructions, and taking listener calls. Dad knew that if news or activity happened that touched the lives of his people, he had to be there.

CHAPTER 4

WHEN I FELL IN LOVE

The one event that completely captured the emotions of the audience and catapulted the *Ron Drake Show* from a successful and highly rated morning drive program to an institution in the community took place in December of 1962. It was nearly three years since the show debuted, and this day would mark the moment I fell in love with radio.

I was finishing a cup of hot chocolate at our kitchen table and listening to Dad comment on the morning's biggest news story. A fire had broken out overnight in Steelton, a town just up the river from Harrisburg. The fire wiped out an expanse of row homes, leaving countless families homeless. My father expressed how sad this was and, since Christmas was only days away, that it would be nice if we could do something for these people. He left it at that, and I went back to my room to finish getting ready for school.

A few minutes later, I was heading out the door to catch the bus to sixth grade. My mom came over to kiss me good-bye, smiling. She told me Mr. Sausman called into the show and donated $500.00 for the people in Steelton. Mr. Sausman was Dave Sausman, the owner of Sausman Chevrolet and one of WHP's largest advertisers.

Eight hours later, as I walked up the sidewalk, I saw my mother standing at our front door with a peculiar look on her face. I wasn't able to read it.

When I walked inside the house, I heard the radios blaring from the kitchen and the living room. "Listen," she said, "Dad's still on the air. The people have been calling all day. After Mr. Sausman's call, it started, and it just keeps going."

The outpouring of concern, love, and generosity from the listeners was overwhelming. All this from a simple comment following the news. What made me fall head over heels in love with radio was seeing for myself the magical relationship between the radio station, the radio performer, and the listener.

Maybe I could have picked it up in conversation, learned about it in a classroom, or read about it in a textbook, but it is hard to think anything could have been more effective than witnessing it first hand and at such a young and impressionable age.

At that moment, I knew that the ability to inform, entertain, and relate was the force behind the power to move people to action and, ultimately, the power to move product. Beyond being able to communicate the attributes and benefits of a product or service, the relationship and trust between the radio station and the audience leads to a special sort of endorsement that is appreciated and welcomed by the listener.

CHAPTER 5

LIVING IN THE MEDIA WORLD

I **was lucky** to grow up as I did and develop thoughts and feelings of my own about media. While the family rode in the car with the radio playing, my parents and I, and later my younger brothers, would talk about what we were hearing, the songs, the selections chosen, the order and the flow, the styles used by the announcers, and the imaging material identifying and positioning the stations. The discussions would be about the purpose and demographic aim of a station.

When watching TV together and looking at the news, the family would talk about story counts, stories selected, and the length of the stories. During the programs, my mother would comment on the quality of the writing and dialogue, using her degree and training as a basis. How the characters were developed and made real was always a topic as well.

Staying current with music, movie, and entertainment news was easy. We always had the latest issues of *Billboard* and *Variety* on our living room coffee table. I was reading trade magazines before I started reading comic books. There was also the occasional spiff.

I remember vividly the night Dad was going through his mail, which included an envelope from Capitol Records. (We still received volumes of promotional mail at home.) Inside was "I Want to Hold Your Hand." There were some simple and fun advantages to growing up the son of a radio personality. Getting advance copies of Beatles records was one of them.

Otherwise, my high school years were pretty much the same as everyone else's. To me it was just Dad's job to be on the radio and entertain, although the hours were strange. Monday through Saturday up at 4:30 a.m. to be on the air from six to ten o'clock—yes, six days a week—as well as Rotary, Kiwanis, and Harrisburg Exchange Club meetings in the afternoons. Evenings and weekends were filled with personal appearances and live broadcasts.

The years rolled along and the *Ron Drake Show* continued to grow in popularity and ratings dominance. Humor and stunts became more prominent; phony news and weather, put-on calls, and April fools were all part of mornings on WHP.

On summer vacations, it was always a treat to take family trips in the car. We'd head down to the Jersey Shore, passing through Philadelphia, listening to WFIL and WIP. On our way up to Connecticut to see my grandparents, we'd listen to New York's WABC, WINS, and WNEW. A little farther up the coast, it was WRKO in Boston. These were the gold standard big market radio stations of the day, exciting, compelling, alive with personality and promotion, and always connected to the local community fan base. These stations were also well financed, all owned by large companies with the resources to support and develop the stations in the radio division.

CHAPTER 6

WORK

When I turned fourteen, I decided it was time to get to work. I loved the idea of earning my own money and creating some degree of financial independence. I applied at our neighborhood McDonald's.

This was perfect for me. The restaurant was an easy walk, about six blocks from home, and I was only fourteen, so by law was not permitted to work at night. I could put in a full day, be off at 7:00 p.m., and have my evenings free.

The tough part was, during the work hours, we really had to work. The franchisee, Richard "Dick" Neenan, was on premises nearly every minute. When he had to leave to run an errand or attend a meeting, his wife, Norma, would take over, and if they had to go somewhere together, they had two adult daughters to look after the place, and they were disciplinarians too. Being in my early teens, I resented the regimen and the discipline, but I realized, later, I learned as much in the fifteen months that I worked at McDonald's as I did in seventeen years in the classroom.

Mr. Neenan poured every cent he had into buying the store. This was one of the early McDonald's, opening in 1962. He had to make it work, and he made sure it, and we, did. Mr. Neenan taught us to make the most of everything. Nothing went to waste. I tried to throw away what I thought was an empty can of chocolate syrup one day, and he showed me how to scrape the sides and the bottom to get every drop out of the can. He said, "Barry, you were about to throw away three milkshakes." An early lesson on operating with thin margins.

My first job was running the milkshake department. The crew made the milkshakes in those days—syrup, milk, and ice milk—all measured to exact specifications and then put on spindles. I'd usually have six or eight going at the same time. The other part of the job was managing the inventory. During high-traffic hours, we would keep twenty shakes at the proper temperature in the refrigerated bins: twelve chocolate, six vanilla, and two strawberry. I learned then that business is all about determining what the customer is going to want and then delivering it, and doing so by maintaining consistent habits of preparation.

After a few months at McDonald's, I was promoted to work the window, greet the customers, take and fill the orders, collect the money, and make change. At first, I thought that the customers were mean. They seemed rushed, angry, and some wouldn't even look at me but, instead, looked up at the electronic menu. I soon understood they weren't mean. They just didn't care about me. All the customers wanted were to get their hamburgers and fries and shut their kids up. My job was to see that it happened, while wearing a big smile and serving the food with that special McDonald's politeness.

CHAPTER 7

RETAIL

When I approached my sixteenth birthday, I left McDonald's and was hired by Feller's Men's Shop downtown. It was fun being downtown in the middle of all the action. The suburbs featured a few small malls and shopping centers, but downtown was still where everyone went to shop, dine, and hang out. Being a part of the scene was great for someone my age, and it gave me my first and lasting lessons in retailing.

The men, and they were all men in 1967, who ran the store were smart, hardworking, and loved what they were doing. The store president, Tom Szilogy, took care of the building lease, finances, tax work, and all the corporate tasks. The merchandise manager, John Ditko, did all of the buying for the store. The floor manager, Dick Wesley, is, to this day, the most talented retail salesman I have ever known. He was able to convey his love of the clothing and persuade the customers to love it too. He was a true showman, and those of us fortunate to work under him all became better as a result. We didn't think of ourselves as floor-walking clerks. We were salesmen.

The retail business was fascinating to observe. The merchandise manager was always six to eight months ahead of the season. He was finished with Christmas and looking ahead to the spring before we put the fall sport coats out.

As much enjoyment as existed in displaying and presenting the merchandise to shoppers, real serious moments occurred, too. Every night at closing time, we'd run the register, i.e., put the cash register through the steps to tally the day's receipts. We'd see the store's total sales for the day and compare it to sales from the same day of the prior year. When we beat the number, we sighed a moment of relief. When we didn't, we got very quiet. That's when we got a dose of reality. We'd look around the store at the stocked shelves and racks knowing that this merchandise had to move. The only way the store could pay for it was to sell it. This is when I developed an understanding and empathy for retailers. It doesn't matter what category (apparel, furniture, appliances, health and beauty aids) or size (the boutique in a small strip center or Wal-Mart, Target, or Macy's). It's all the same.

To learn all this while still a kid in school was a big advantage for me. I enjoyed my two years at the store, and even though I went off to Penn State in 1969, I still returned, helped out, and put in some hours during the Christmas and back-to-school seasons.

When I came in to work the Christmas season of my junior year in college, I was told it would be the last. Following the post-Christmas sale in January and the winter clearance in February, Feller's Men's Store was closing. Time to get an advanced education in retail as I learned the reasons.

Two key people moved on. Mr. Ditko left to open a store of his own about sixty miles away. This was a blow because his skill at blending art and science was difficult to match.

Shortly after that, the store's tailor, Pete, left to start his own shop. His technical skills were replaced, but his warmth and trust were now missing. Pete was a key player on the team, and the customers noticed his absence.

On top of what was going on inside the store, there was now two to three times the retail square footage in the suburbs compared to five years prior. Downtown customer traffic counts were off considerably.

Combining all of the above with inflation, the rising rates of lease space and employee costs (even minimum wage had gone up several times), and the looming 1973-1975 recession and its 9 percent unemployment, Feller's was left with extremely limited maneuverability. Liquidation was determined as the only viable option.

The president handled the process with speed and efficiency. Dick Wesley went on to start his own business, serving an exclusive clientele with high-end men's clothing, proving tremendously successful. I drove back up to State College to finish my junior year at Penn State and started working part time in, of all things, radio.

PART TWO
THE OLD DAYS

CHAPTER 8

STARTING OUT

Monday, June 4, 1973. Day one of my forty years. I started out hosting the midday show, 10:00 a.m. to 2:00 p.m., on WCPA-900AM Clearfield, Pennsylvania. I had just graduated from Penn State and thought myself fortunate to be employed. I got the job in Clearfield because the stations were owned by the same company that owned the stations in State College where I had been working part time while going to school. The principal was William "Bill" Ulrich. He owned the newspaper in Clearfield, along with the town's only AM and FM radio stations. AM was still dominating radio at this time. WCPA's format was Top40, although a very adult-flavored version. The manager, Carl, was hesitant to play any music he thought might offend Mr. Ulrich. The AM was the moneymaker. The FM played easy listening instrumentals and almost no commercials.

I only met Mr. Ulrich once. It was late on a Sunday afternoon, and I was getting ready to go home after a six-hour air shift. I noticed an old guy wandering around the parking lot looking lost. "May I help you, sir?" I asked, poking my head out the door. He said, "No, just looking around." He appeared harmless, so I locked the front door and went back to the studio to put my stuff away. Next thing I know, this man was walking down the hallway. "How did you get in here?" I yelped. He just smiled and chuckled and said, "Oh, I have a key." All I could do was stare at him, and then he realized I didn't know who he was. "It's OK," he assured me. "I'm Bill Ulrich." That was the only time I saw Mr. Ulrich in my nearly two years in Clearfield. To me, he was exactly what the owner of a station should look like. At that time, I thought there were two types of owners in the radio business: big corporations, such as CBS, RCA, and Westinghouse, or old men (who must be wealthy).

It really wasn't any concern of mine who owned WCPA. I was just happy to be working in radio and learning how a station operated. The beauty of working at a station like WCPA was getting to do everything. In addition to the midday show, I read the news during afternoon drive, 3:00-6:00 p.m., and did commercial production in between time. Four or five of us worked on-air at WCPA. On the weekends, besides a Saturday or Sunday on-air shift, we'd take turns doing high school sports, live broadcasts from sponsor locations, and hosting events such as holiday parades and the Clearfield County Fair.

Due to the nature of a small town, everyone in Clearfield knew who the announcers on the radio station were. In a few weeks, I started noticing people would say hello to me by name as I walked around downtown.

Another benefit to working in a small community was getting to know all the stations' advertisers. It wasn't that I set out to meet them. It just happened. Sometimes a meeting took place as part of official business, an advertiser might want some special help with a commercial, or the station was doing a live appearance or broadcast from their store. Other times it was merely social. We'd all see each other in restaurants or other public places. The clients felt we were doing important work, and, as broadcasters, were in a position to exert influence. The local business people valued having a positive relationship with the radio stations and the stations' employees.

After about a year at the station, the GM named me program director, an important responsibility, as the other announcers now reported to me, and I was in charge of selecting the music for the station to play. I found myself enjoying this job more than just being on the air. I interacted daily with the general manager and the salesmen. While I had no direct selling duties, I was involved in designing the stations' promotional packages for the sales staff and developing special programs, such as our year-end countdown show, and creating sponsorship opportunities for the advertisers. I enjoyed listening to the feedback the sales staff got from our clients, and I felt heartened when told of an advertiser's success and, at the same time, challenged when an advertising campaign did not fare as well as a client had hoped.

One night my phone rang, and on the other end of the line was a friend I had worked with during college, "Wild Bill." He was now the program director of WLYC-AM and WILQ-FM in Williamsport, PA, about two hours to the east. Bill wanted to know if I'd come work for him, doing middays on WLYC, news in the afternoon on WILQ, and commercial production. Sound familiar? I thanked him but said, "Bill, I'm the program director here now and enjoying it." He said, "Well I can't make you program director because I'm the program director, but I'll make you the music director." The Williamsport market population was bigger than the Clearfield market, so this would be a move up for me. Plus, the money was more than I was making, so I said yes, put all my belongings in my car, and took off down Route 80.

CHAPTER 9

THE NEW OWNERS

A bout a month after I moved to Williamsport, Wild Bill showed up at my apartment one night and said, "We need to talk." I expected the worst, something like format change, and we're all out. Instead, Bill told me the stations had been sold, and he wanted me to hear the news directly from him. I felt it was nice the program director came to visit with this information, but I was still just happy to be working in radio and not very interested in who owned the stations.

Two weeks later, I stood in the studio just after 11:30 in the morning, thinking about my next witticism and the timing of the upcoming song's intro ramp, when in walked Henry, our general manager, with two relatively young men. I was twenty-three, and the two men looked to me to be about ten years older. "Barry," the GM said, "I'd like you to meet the new owners." We shook hands, exchanged short pleasantries, and then I said, "Thank you for coming in but, if you'll excuse me, I'm on the air." I put my headphones on and turned away to get back to work. I had never met the stations' current owner. I couldn't imagine why it would matter to me that I know the new owners.

The two gentlemen were Kerby Confer and Paul Rothfuss. What they didn't mention during our short introduction was they would be working at the stations every day. Kerby and Paul moved into an office together, desks facing each other, and were co-general managers, co-sales managers, and spent much of each day out on the street seeing clients and prospects. The two were former on-air radio disc jockeys who several years earlier had made the move into sales at WYRE-AM in Annapolis, Maryland. There they learned the business side of radio and were hit with a bug to own a station themselves. When the opportunity came up in their hometown of Williamsport, they jumped at it. Not since watching my father while growing up did I see two guys so excited about coming to work every day. Kerby and Paul's energy and enthusiasm inspired the salespeople—yes, we had four women on the team. Society was evolving very quickly in that mid-1970's period. (Maybe due to the success of the *Mary Tyler Moore Show*.) Radio sales was a terrific opportunity for women to enter and move up in the workforce. No special background or degree was required, and pay was based on performance.

The revenue at WLYC/WILQ grew substantially. I could tell because I was running more commercials in my show, and commercial copywriting and production were taking up more and more of the on-air team's time. All of us were moving at a frenetic pace.

Four months of this hyper activity and Wild Bill headed for the exits. I still don't know exactly what took place, but one afternoon my old friend was just gone and the next morning I was named program director.

Once again, I felt the enjoyment of being involved in everything. I still had my show, chose all the music for WLYC-AM, and designed the format clocks, but now I also was attending sales meetings and working more closely with management.

Salespeople began to ask me to join them on calls. Because I was the program director, the salespeople used my title to impress the clients. Also, the salespeople wanted me to hear the clients' business objectives and have more information in order to create a better commercial.

Kerby and Paul believed in using commercials as a sales tool. They taught the salespeople that when they had a commercial ready to play for prospects (specs) that prospects were more likely to buy. They also emphasized getting results for the clients. Kerby always said, "The best prospects to buy more advertising are your current customers—when they are happy." The salespeople learned that when clients begin to run a campaign they want to feel action and response right away. In every sales meeting Paul would declare, "Make sure something happens in the store when the commercials run on the air."

During that time, the owners continued working at high energy levels but appeared less stressed and even started talking about expansion. I was not privy to the company's financial statements, but there was one piece of data about which I did learn.

As I was spending increased amounts of time in the owners' office, I couldn't help but notice a four-square-inch piece of white paper taped to the top of each desk. On that paper was written a series of numbers.

My curiosity aroused, I got to the point where I couldn't control myself and one day, while sitting in the office with the owners, I just blurted out, "What is this? I see this paper and this number every time I'm in here. The number doesn't change, the paper never moves, and there is never anything on top of it blocking your view. What is it?"

Kerby and Paul just looked at each other without saying anything at all. In retrospect, I think they were trying to decide if it was OK to talk to me about it.

Paul stood up and quietly closed the office door. When he sat back down, he and Kerby looked at each other again. Kerby slowly began to explain, "Paul and I, as individuals, were able to make some investment in these radio stations, but the bulk of the money to make the purchase was borrowed, most from the bank (literally across the street) and the remainder from the prior owner—seller paper. It's just like when you buy a house and take out a mortgage. The real owners are not the people living in the house but the finance company. Paul and I are personally on the hook for these loans."

I understood. Kerby and Paul may have been the "owners" according to the FCC, but the financial performance of the stations was essential to their being able to repay the bank loan and the amount the previous owner had financed for them.

Paul paused slightly, then stated, "This number on the paper is the revenue we must produce in the first year in order to keep the radio stations."

The impact was chilling. I was frozen. Talk about putting it all on the line. This is no carnival. This is serious business.

I realized that this situation was so completely different from anything I had ever been involved with before. I wasn't working for a corporation. The owners weren't old rich men. Kerby and Paul were two guys with a dream, and two guys not that much older than I was. At that moment, the seed was planted. Someday I could own a radio station.

CHAPTER 10

HITTING THE STREETS

Several months later, I was on the phone with Croy Pitzer, the manager of WMAJ in State College, who I worked for while going to Penn State. We were having a friendly catch-up "Happy New Year" chat when he told me one of his salesmen was leaving the market, which created a big hole to fill. "Do you know anyone who might want this job?" he asked. "Sure," I said. "Me."

I had spent enough time with salespeople and advertisers over the past four years to know that I could do the job. More important, I had been thinking more and more about the idea of one day owning a radio station. To get to that point, I figured I would have to become a general manager. To have any credibility, I knew it was necessary to have actual experience as a radio salesman. I would need to know what it's really all about to make a living on the street selling advertising and dealing with the clients. The next week, I went over to State College, met with the stations' sales manager and business manager, and committed to joining the sales staff. Croy and I shook hands to cement the deal.

Since I worked in casual on-air radio attire every day, there was just one suit in my closet, from my wedding day the prior spring. I dusted it off and went out and bought a second so I could alternate day to day. With that, a few ties and a shoeshine, I was all set on March 7, 1977, for my new job as a salesman at WMAJ-AM and WXLR-FM in State College, Pennsylvania.

There was no formal sales training program at WMAJ. The sales manager, Tod, was also the morning personality. He had to handle accounts and be the sales manager much the same way the high school football coach has to teach history and be the school's guidance counselor.

Since this was a university town, the stores were filled with books about business: sales, marketing, management. Every night after dinner, I would read for a few hours to teach myself my new craft. Studying like this helped me get in the right frame of mind for working in sales but in no way offered a complete education. Most of my education came from the business people I called on during the day. These business owners helped me by talking to me, telling me why they were buying and what they were trying to accomplish. I went to one of my bigger clients, The HI-FI House, with an idea for a traffic-building promotion. The owner told me, "I don't want traffic. Traffic wastes my time. I want to advertise to the few with the money and appreciation for a good stereo." I learned the pitfalls right away about pitching station promotions that may be good for the station but of no interest to the advertiser. And I also got a good lesson on how selective reach is more important to many businesses than mass reach.

Other clients helped me; knowing their merchandise, they showed me how to put together better commercials. I worked on a campaign with a lawn and garden store for Bolens Mulching Mowers. Trust me that I knew nothing about these machines. The owner of the store took me through the specific benefits of owning the mower, points a homeowner with a sizeable plot of land would appreciate. These small details made a big difference in the effectiveness of the commercial we created.

Then there were those who helped me by being tough, or just flat-out rude. They'd refuse to see me, or insult me, or speak negatively about radio or my stations. This helped because I had to figure out how to win them over. The Boalsburg Steakhouse was a prospect I had a tough time cracking. The owner just wouldn't see me. I started eating lunch there once a week (I had to eat somewhere). I made no attempt to talk to him. I just came in, sat down, and enjoyed a good sandwich. One day after about nine weeks, the owner came over to my table and said, "OK, what do you want?" He turned into a regular advertiser on WMAJ.

The other salespeople helped me too. A few veterans took the time to talk with me about their experiences and road to success. They noticed I had a capacity for hard work, and I think they figured that if I would bring in a few new accounts it would keep the managers off their backs. The person who ended up helping me the most was Ken, a salesperson hired shortly after I was.

There was a small leather goods store, Sundance Leather. It was on my prospect list, businesses I was supposed to be working on to turn into clients. I stopped into Sundance once or twice but never felt much warmth from the person there, and I deemed the business too small and too disinterested for me to call on them anymore, and I just forgot about them.

Then one Friday night at the station, I was looking at the production bulletin board. This was where the list of the clients who had commercials in production was posted. That night, on the board was a production order for Sundance Leather. Ken, the new guy, had made the sale to a business I thought was not worth my time. I was embarrassed. I was angry. Most of all, I was determined that this was never again going to happen to me. It is often said that attitude trumps aptitude. I can't say my aptitude for sales improved, but this incident set my attitude straight. Never again would I let a prospect slip away. Never would I throw in the towel before trying everything and exhausting all possibilities. Never again would I fail to do the work. The new guy taught me one important lesson, one of the most valuable sales training sessions I ever had.

CHAPTER 11
FM

Tod, the morning man/sales manager, called a meeting of the WMAJ-AM/WXLR-FM sales staff. We didn't get together very often as a group. The last time our staff assembled, management announced it intended to reduce our commission rates. The two top salespeople cried foul and threatened to leave. Management quickly abandoned the plan (an early lesson in labor relations). So when a meeting was called we all felt some anxiety. What new idea had management cooked up now?

Croy and Tod walked into the meeting room, and Tod shouted, "You are a poor excuse for a sales staff." He said we were a bunch of goof-offs because we weren't selling the FM. All the effort was devoted to the AM, and very few clients and very few dollars were going to FM.

WMAJ-AM, having signed on in 1945, was a heritage, full-service station: news, play-by-play sports, personalities, and contests. WMAJ-AM had many ways to involve clients with the station: live commercials, sponsorships, and dozens of packages to attract advertisers. The sales team found lots to talk about on sales calls. After hearing an explanation of what WMAJ was offering at the moment, however, the prospect typically showed little interest in listening to a presentation on the FM station. The salespeople had a fire and passion for WMAJ. This enthusiasm did not exist for the FM, WXLR. The AM was buyer friendly, and most sales calls resulted in an order. So being typical salespeople, we took the easy way out, not wanting to rock the boat, and forgot about the FM.

Now the sales team was being scolded and told we had to start getting orders for the FM, or else. No one ever said what the "or else" was going to be. Management didn't want to push things too far after the fiasco at the last meeting.

The sales manager told us to continue to sell as we had been, but, after securing the AM order, to ask in the do-you-want-fries-with-that style for an additional order for the FM. His thinking was that if each salesperson did that on every call, even if only one in five or one in ten resulted in an FM order, the business would grow.

The logic was sound. The execution was a disgrace. The idea never got off the ground. I tried the technique a few times and I'm sure the other salespeople did too, but I never did it regularly enough for it to be a habit. In a short while, I stopped doing it altogether.

I take and deserve the blame here, but the lesson I learned was that when salespeople are left to their own devices, anything can, or in this case can't, happen. There was no monitoring. A manager never went out with me and watched me on a sales call. If one had, maybe I would have built some confidence in asking for the FM and maybe have gotten to the point of comfortably doing it regularly. The idea may have worked, but there was no serious follow-up. No one was minding the store. I remembered the training I received at McDonald's where there were exact procedures to follow for everything. We were taught exactly how to fill an order: cold drinks first, hot food next, fries always last. What made the procedure take hold, however, was management being on the floor, watching our every move. Management can teach and train all day long, but there is no substitute for being there.

After a couple of months, and seeing no progress at all with the initiative to sell the FM, Croy called me into his office. "What's wrong with the station?" he asked. "Is there a problem with the programming?"

"Absolutely nothing is wrong with the programming on WXLR," I answered. "All my friends listen to the station. I hear positive comments from people all the time. The business people in town believe WXLR is a good station; many merchants are playing it in their stores. The trouble is," I went on, "that while the format is separate from WMAJ-AM, as is the programming staff, both stations are using the same sales staff. Our salespeople are AM salespeople. The salespeople are known by the clients as the WMAJ salespeople. We are identified as the AM people. We believe in it and are well schooled in its qualities, attributes, and benefits. This sales staff just doesn't possess the same emotion for WXLR and so doesn't have the capacity to sell a second station." (This was a perfect example of why I felt it so crucial to go into radio sales and learn it from practical experience. I knew why we were coming up short on the FM station because I was out on the street myself. All I had to do was look in the mirror to assess the situation.)

Abruptly, the GM said he had to leave to go take care of something and showed me the door. Though our meeting had come to a sudden end, I kept thinking about our FM for days.

WXLR-FM was labeled soft rock. It was a steady diet of the Eagles, Jackson Brown, Laura Nyro, Joni Mitchell, Crosby, Stills and Nash, as well as some current pop hits from artists like Fleetwood Mac, Chicago, and Billy Joel. The playlist was hip enough for young adults but mellow enough for the older crowd. The presentation was low key, with minimal talk, and the station aired very few commercials.

I began to believe that, with proper attention, WXLR-FM could generate at least half the monthly revenue of WMAJ-AM. I also knew the GM was not going to authorize additional expenditures to hire a sales staff, betting on future income. It was then that I devised a plan to take over sales of the FM.

The plan allowed me to continue selling and servicing the business I was responsible for on WMAJ-AM and to manage the sales of the FM, in addition. Two announcers on the WXLR programming staff showed an interest and aptitude for sales, so I hired them to sell part time. The arrangement was they'd keep their programming salaries and then be paid commission on their FM sales. The GM and I worked out a deal so that I could earn an override commission on FM sales, in addition to the commissions I was earning on my sales of the AM. Since this plan called for no additional fixed costs, and any extra revenue would be nearly all added profit, the GM OK'd trying it. As 1978 approached, I was filled with excitement and anticipation about what could be accomplished with WXLR.

Getting together with my two part-time salespeople, we put together a strategy. We decided we wanted to be different from the other radio stations in town. WXLR salespeople would not go out and pitch spots and precanned packages. Instead, we would make an initial call with a readied list of questions to learn what our prospects were trying to achieve and then come back with a custom proposal.

Immediately, business people took to this approach. The prospects felt that going through the questions we had prepared was a help in the planning and budgeting of their business and liked the seriousness of the method. At the same time, because the WXLR salespeople were experienced in copywriting and production, we were able to come up with new commercial ideas for our prospects. These commercials were tailor-made to be effective with the WXLR listener. Also, the station vowed to keep the commercial load low so that the advertisers would feel exclusive. All the others, AM and FM, were running eighteen to twenty-four commercial units an hour, so WXLR being at half that was a noticeable point of difference.

After the new sales team succeeded in getting a few clients on the air, it was time to ice the cake. WXLR was "sold out." The three of us would carefully explain to the clients and prospects that, due to high demand and the terrific results WXLR was producing for the advertisers, there were no commercial availabilities. "Yes," we would say, "we can accommodate you next week or next month, but right now we are sold out."

This shocked the clients. No radio station in the market had ever told prospective advertisers that there was no vacancy. Oh, maybe for a day or two at Christmas time or back to school, or during the political season, but never on a regular basis. The story was believable because the clients could hear the air personalities and promotional announcements on the air selling the benefits of fewer commercials and more music.

Being "sold out" put WXLR in a new light. The station developed an aura, a mystique, and this played into the natural desire people have to want what is unattainable. I slowly but steadily raised the prices we were charging. As primitive as it was, the station was using an inventory/rate management system that took advantage of supply and demand.

One of my part-timers was doing so well that he quit his day job and became a full-time salesperson. Just a few months later, the station added another full-time person to the sales staff. WXLR's full-year revenue target was surpassed by midsummer. I was proud of what we accomplished in a short period. The advertisers appreciated our attention to their business needs and how we took responsibility for running campaigns that produced tangible results. I saw here what Kerby and Paul had preached in Williamsport: how much the clients value a good commercial, *good* defined as one that produces specific action.

CHAPTER 12

ACCOUNTABILITY

Today there is much talk about the advertiser's desire to hold the media accountable. It is said that in this tight economy, with competition as tough as ever, the media must be able to deliver demonstrable results. After forty thousand calls, I have to laugh. This is something new? One of my first clients explained the facts of life to me early in my forty years.

It was Ishler's Furniture. Norm Ishler, the store's owner, and I had been working together for several months, and the revenue from this client had grown to the point that the store was now one of my top three billing accounts. I sat down with Norm one morning to put the finishing touches on the commercial copy for the upcoming summer clearance sale. The budget and the schedule had already been decided, so I knew, that as Norm spoke, he wasn't trying to be clever or negotiate a better deal. He just stopped me before we said good-bye and, in a very soft but stern voice, told me, "Barry, these commercials have got to work." I didn't say a word. No time for cheap sales talk here. I just looked back into my client's eyes, took his hand firmly, said "thank you," and walked out the door. We understood each other perfectly. To successfully realize our self-interests, we depended on one another. That is what is meant by the term *relationship*.

The fact was the new fall merchandise was already on the way and set to arrive over the next two weeks. Payment was due. The sale had to generate the cash to make those payments. It was important for me, as an advertising salesman, to get this message and know I was being held accountable. In true business relationships, accountability has always been the priority.

CHAPTER 13

A New (?) Idea

Radio station people pride themselves on coming up with ideas for clients, but often the clients come up with amazing ones.

One of my clients had an idea to do ten-second commercials. That, in and of itself, was nothing new. Our stations always had a few short ads on the air. His idea, however, was to do a very simple piece of copy. The first line would describe a specific item the store wanted to highlight, then would come the name of the store and short address.

"Who has Pappagallo shoes for women starting at $38? Kalin's, 135 South Allen Street."

What and where. The copy was set; there were a couple dozen different pieces, each containing just one item. But it was the schedule that made this campaign a winner.

The schedule called for one ten-second commercial each hour, twenty-four hours a day, seven days a week. After just a few days, the station began to get requests from our current advertisers, and from businesses we had never heard from before, looking for the kind of impact this campaign was generating. Of course, it was the good copy and dominating schedule that caused the impact.

The general manager was intelligent about this. He knew this was a hot idea, but also knew the on-air product had to be protected. How many of these short commercials could a station air before it became a listener tune-out and therefore counterproductive?

The GM established a policy to allow the station to run two ten-second commercials an hour, thirty minutes apart. These commercials were available only to clients buying the entire day, i.e., twenty-four commercials, one each hour. The program was called "Headliners." Twenty-four tens over twenty-four hours, pick your day(s). This enabled the station to preserve a quality sound. The clients received a high vertical frequency schedule dominating a day. The advertisers saw results, and, because there were only availabilities for two clients each day, the station had a waiting list.

CHAPTER 14

SMART CLIENTS

Another client who had an idea that put extra commission in my check owned several restaurants in town. Andy Zangrilli's line up of eateries covered it all, including a fancy place with tablecloths, Dante's, the casual HiWay Pizza, a delicatessen, and a bar. Andy ran commercials promoting his brand name and just listed the different restaurants under that umbrella.

Although Andy was the biggest local restaurant operator in town, he felt vulnerable when hearing other restaurants promoting unique single brands against his group. For example, two or three other fine dining establishments advertised, and even though Andy was spending more, his fine dining message for Dante's wasn't cutting through, as it was only a part of his commercial. Eventually, Andy came to the conclusion that the method he was using was costing him business.

The budget was entirely reworked, taking the single expenditure for the group and putting almost that same amount to work for each individual restaurant. Now each restaurant in his group had its own commercial and its own campaign. Instantly, my revenue from this client was increased by three-and-a-half times. Happy days for me and happy days for my client, too. The income from each restaurant soared, easily covering the increased advertising expense, resulting in higher profits, and Andy was delighted knowing he was keeping his competitors from gaining on him. It's always an advantage when the salesperson has smart clients to work with.

CHAPTER 15

TIME OUT

Special Report #1: The Commercial

Imagine a customer walking into a shoe store to buy new shoes and the racks and shelves are empty. The greeter asks, "May I help you?" The customer can't say "just looking" because there is nothing to look at. So maybe the customer says something about wanting to buy new shoes. At that point, the clerk says, "We have shoes from $150 a pair to $600 a pair. What do you want to spend?" Still not comprehending, the customer answers, "Ahh, $250." "Wonderful," says the storekeeper, "will that be cash or charge? I'll ring you up over here." "Whoa," the customer cries, "what about the shoes? I haven't seen any, much less tried any on." The storekeeper grins and replies, "I will get you a good pair of shoes as soon as you pay me the $250." My bet is the customer would hightail it out the door and never go into that store again.

This story is preposterous, but it's based on something radio salespeople try to do every day. That is, try to sell radio without audio. No one would buy the shoes without seeing them first. Even online shoppers view pictures of the merchandise they are ordering. Consumers are allowed to sample two minutes of a song before clicking Buy on iTunes. Why would anyone buy a radio schedule without hearing the commercial?

Here is a real world story about the value of audio, and it directly relates to the radio business. It's about music production companies that created and sold branding IDs for radio stations called "jingles." Some of the material was made up of short bursts of simply the station call letters: Double You Kay Bee Double You! Others included station descriptors as well: MUSICRADIO Double You ELLL ESSS! Some would be longer, with lyrics about the community and the lifestyle of the marketplace. These musical images were used to embellish a radio station's character and to position a station relative to a competitor. The creators of these jingles employed salesmen to go into the field and visit station managers and program directors to present the latest offerings. I was in several of these meetings when I first became a program director. The salesmen came in armed with audience data on stations using the jingles. The statistics were shown to convince station management that playing these jingles between the songs on their station would make the station's ratings go up. After making this logical argument, the salesmen would play samples of the work. With each burst of brass and bass, the station personnel would get more thrilled, imagining how great the station was going to sound and how profits would rise on the back of the higher ratings. The checkbook would come out, the down payment made, contract signed, and a date would be set for the orchestra and chorus to produce the full package. The manager would gleefully sign the deal with all the optimism that the station's future, and his own, were now secure.

This story is important because no business could transact without the jingle salesman's demonstration. It is hearing the demonstration and the sound that creates the emotion. Action and decision making are a result of emotion. All the logic, the data, the statistical arguments fall flat until they are seasoned with feelings.

To ask for action, to ask for a decision, to ask for a commitment, to expect an order, a salesperson must first capture the prospect's imagination and ignite a feeling. That is the value of playing audio for prospects.

入

When radio people go out to sell and go without audio, the process is upside down and backwards, and that's why salespeople hear an emphatic NO 90 percent of the time.

When a presentation is made to a prospect, even when including the best of logical reasons why the prospect should buy, and the salesperson does not present audio, any reasonable expectation for closing the sale is greatly diminished. The prospect may not say it aloud, but I know, from forty thousand calls, that silently they are asking themselves, "How would I do this? How will I get a commercial? How will it be written? What is the cost of such a project?" What they say aloud is, "Very interesting. I appreciate you coming by, and I will be giving this serious consideration. Run along now."

Coverage maps, zip code analyses, ratings, qualitative studies, consumer buying data, all great stuff to have. Audio. Sound. The Commercial. That is the number one tool. The commercial is all about the prospect's business. That is what the prospect really cares about.

After discovering the prospect's objective and putting it together in sound, it makes clear to the prospect what will run, and how the campaign will be executed. Hearing the commercial for their business and their name, their selling points, offers and benefits will bring the prospect's emotion to the forefront.

⅄

The arts, crafts, and gift store Uncle Eli's was an on-again, off-again user of radio and our stations. Doug, the owner, would routinely place a schedule for certain seasonal events throughout the year. I had been in the store enough times to get to know the merchandise, so I started to put together commercials for Uncle Eli's, and I'd take them into the store to play for Doug. At first, he was critical. "I'll call you when I want to run something," he'd say. Then after a while, he started listening to the commercials and critiqued the copy. As soon as he did this, I knew I was on the right track. Doug was beginning to get emotional and getting into the process. Soon, he was making just a few comments on the copy and asking to get the commercial on the air. Uncle Eli's began advertising each month, not just occasionally, and upped the advertising investment as the store's business improved. Doug was a happy client who only got happier as he ran more substantial and more frequent campaigns, all driven by his hearing new commercial ideas.

⅄

With all the competition for attention while in the prospect's office or store, bells and buzzers going off, screens to glance at, it's a constant struggle to keep someone focused on a sales presentation.

The best money I ever spent in my forty years was buying a good-sounding cassette player (no digital devices in 1977). When I'd walk into a sales call, I was confident of gaining attention and moving the process forward because all I had to do was push the button and let my cassette player do the work. I had a fool-proof method to keep the prospect engaged. Sound.

Presenting with sound cuts through the competition for attention and zeroes in on what the prospect truly cares about: their objective and mission. Such is the case in Chicago, Charlotte, and Cheyenne.

CHAPTER 16

TIME OUT

Special Report #2: Commercial Copy

R adio salespeople live inside radio stations. The salespeople interact with copywrit-ers and commercial producers all the time. Salespeople in radio listen to com-mercials in meetings, play commercials for one another, and experience com-mercials very differently than the average radio listener.

The prospects radio salespeople call on are all consumed with their own businesses: the merchandise they buy and sell, the rent they have to pay, the credit policies of their stores, and their competitors. These prospects devote very little time, if any at all, to radio commercial production.

Business owners are exposed to commercials as they listen to the radio, but radio clients and prospects listening to commercials are like me when I look at the moon at night. I don't know what it's made of, how it was made, or how it got up there. I just admire the view.

To work effectively with clients on commercial copy, it's essential to under-stand what I call the roots of retail. (I use the term *retail*, which conjures up im-ages of bricks and mortar and floor space and shelves, but all the concepts here are easily transferred to online retailing and the marketing of services.)

While most of my education comes from the forty thousand calls over the forty years, regarding commercial content, it started much earlier.

On a slow summer afternoon in 1968, I was out on the Feller's Men's Store sales floor trying to look busy when the merchandise manager, Mr. Ditko, suddenly ran down the steps carrying a box. Wearing a big wide smile, he shouted, "Guys, take a look at these shirts I bought. They're called Tom Jones shirts. This one is white, but we'll have them in blue and pink too."

In retail, it's all about the item. The John Ditkos of the world spend all of their time searching for items they believe will connect with their stores' customers. Putting items on display that will attract the customer's interest, getting people talking and, of course, selling at full price sums up the merchant's passion.

The emotion for the merchandise is what drives the merchant to a buying decision. Remember, a retailer is a buyer not a seller. Yes, the merchandise must be sold, but the art of retailing is making the proper buying decisions. What to buy, how much, and at what cost. The merchant makes dozens of decisions a day, sometimes dozens an hour, and deals only in specifics, including volume and cost, color and fabric, delivery time, return policy, etc. With a mind such as this, a radio salesperson can't hope to expect a favorable decision on a proposal to buy radio advertising unless the commercial is prepared and its content is on the mark.

There are just a few basics to learn. Here are just two to get the process started.

Number one: sixties are better than thirties. I know there are occasions with good reasons to use thirties and tens, but they are exceptions. When you are dehydrated, a sixteen-ounce bottle of water is better than an eight-ounce bottle.

Number two: the main character in the commercial is the item. It may be the Tom Jones shirt or a dining room table or a chainsaw. This is what the client wants to hear the commercial talking about, and this is what the radio listener is interested in hearing about. The item will attract the listeners to the store. An effective commercial shines the spotlight on the main character, the item.

Where average closing ratios for most radio salespeople wallow in the one to nine percent range, when sound is included in the presentation and the content is right, the closing ratios regularly approach 50 percent.

With properly written and targeted commercials, a station's accountability scores soar. The station is now able to deliver measurable, tangible results for the advertiser, success that leads to renewals.

Better commercials lead to better results for the advertiser, stronger renewal rates, higher closing ratios for the salesperson, and a better business model for the radio station.

The staff at WXLR came up with a game to play that led to better copy and commercials more effective for the advertisers. All that is needed to play is an ear and the ability to answer two questions honestly. The game can be played anywhere: at home, at work, or in the car.

Whenever a commercial comes on, as a listener ask, what exactly am I supposed to do? When the answer calls for a specific action, score a plus. Any doubt or question, score a minus. Performing this exercise can be a very simple way to grade commercials and to learn to write properly.

Another way to do it takes a bit more imagination but is worth the effort. Again, listen to the commercial, and at the end, ask, if I were the advertiser, what would I expect to happen? If I were spending my own money to run this, what would I want to see? These little games are easy to play and, played repeatedly and scored honestly, are a great assist to writers and producers of commercial content.

Playing these games will take emphasis away from a commercial's window dressing (the fabulous special effects, music, and the sound of the announcer's voice) and put the emphasis where it belongs: motivating the listener and creating action for the advertiser.

CHAPTER 17

ON TO THE MAJORS

With business at WXLR sailing along, our general manager, Croy, was anticipating Bill Parke's annual summer visit to State College. Bill had worked for Croy years earlier. Croy told me he thought it would be a good idea for us to meet. This is when I met Bill Parke, the VP/general manager of WIFI-92FM in Philadelphia.

The introduction on that summer afternoon in State College led to my visiting Philadelphia for an official job interview with Bill, as well as the general sales manager, Frank Tenore, and the executive vice president/radio, John Tenaglia. WIFI-92 was owned by General Cinema Corporation, the movie theatre company, and was the flagship station of the radio division. Tenaglia and the group program director had their offices there. WIFI also served as a feeder to other stations in the group. The previous sales manager was promoted to GM in Chicago. His successor was subsequently moved to Boston, and WIFI's top salesperson ended up being the sales manager in Chicago.

Bill Parke always stayed on the hunt for fresh sales talent. After the interviews, I was hired as salesperson number eight, the new position established to fuel future growth. I started as number eight in September of 1978. By October, I was number seven, November, number six, and December, number five. It wouldn't be accurate for me to claim my rise was due to stellar performance. It was all because of movement and attrition. I mentioned the top salesperson moved to Chicago, then one of the veterans burned out and left. Then the station created a local sales manager position and promoted a strong direct seller. So with each event, I moved up a rung.

WIFI-92 was a Top40 FM. The term contemporary hit radio, CHR, had not been invented yet. The station was tightly focused on 12-34 year-olds with concentration on females 12-24. WIFI dethroned the market's teen-leading heritage Top40 AM, WFIL. That may sound like a no-brainer today, but thirty-five years ago those Top40 AMs were still very entrenched. It had taken WIFI three years to become number one with teens and now the station was competitive among adults 18-34 and 18-49, too.

One of the station's listener benefits, as with all FMs at the time, was its self-controlled commercial load. WIFI ran a maximum of eight minutes and twelve commercial units per hour. The policy was nonnegotiable. Unlike my past experience at WXLR, where we acted "sold out" but could always add inventory if necessary, when WIFI was sold out it was sold out.

I ran into this about six weeks on the job when I got my first order, The New Jersey Bartenders School. After working with the owner to make the sale and have him write a check for the total amount, I proudly walked into the GSM's office with the order in hand. I could barely contain my excitement while my manager nonchalantly glanced at the form, tossed it into his out tray, and glibly remarked, "We'll see if it clears." My mind started spinning. My inside voice cried, "What? See if it clears? You mean I've been out there selling, working like mad to get business, and there may not even be time to run these commercials?" I stopped breathing just long enough to have an out-of-body experience. Looking down at the scene from above, I quickly determined that if I were going to survive and eke out a living at WIFI, I was going to have to get up earlier and work faster.

What I did moving forward from that day was ensure the sales assistant, traffic director, and business manager were on my team. I sent them thank-you notes, flowers, restaurant gift certificates, whatever I could think of to keep me in their hearts. It helped me have an edge, helped move my orders to the top of the stack.

The rates were set by management, so I had no leeway there. Moreover, since all my accounts were new to the station, they had to pay cash in advance.

The business manager reported directly to corporate, so there was no getting around her. I was competing with seven other sales people, and national (which ate up two or three minutes in most hours), for these precious eight commercial minutes. I learned right away that there was competition outside the station and competition inside the station, too.

⋏

Coming to Philadelphia, I had a preconceived notion that there would be a comprehensive sales training program. I was right, but not in the way I imagined. What I anticipated was a planned academic study that would somehow transform me into a more complete salesman. What the introductory program turned out to be was two days of sitting in the sales office—reading. I had two files to go through. One contained copies of written presentations the salespeople had done over the years. Just about every category was covered, and reading the material quickly gave me a good sense of how to explain the value of the station and the station's audience. Reviewing these presentations was also good because I could see how the station went about recommending scheduling, creating copy, and determining rates. Having already had a few years' experience in radio sales, I knew quite a bit about how to schedule radio commercials effectively for clients, but there are always different and better methods, so it was a plus for me to study. For anyone hired by the station who had not been in radio before, this time spent looking at sample proposals would be an even larger benefit.

The other file to read through, again arranged by business category, contained success letters and testimonials written by advertisers. This method of introducing the station to new employees was good psychology at work. Imagine sitting for the better part of a day looking at nothing but glowing reports on the radio station's ability to achieve results for clients. All different types of clients, too: from car dealers to sporting goods retailers, furniture and appliance stores to electronic stores and banks, all writing about their positive experience in dealing with the station.

After being handcuffed to the desk for two days, the next week or so was spent riding with other salespeople. Here I witnessed all that I'd been reading about come to life. I rode shotgun as salespeople navigated through the sprawling seven county metro citing opportunities and deciding when and where to stop the car and cold call.

WIFI salespeople always had five or six set appointments each day, but time remained in between these calls. I learned to make use of the time by stopping into businesses cold and introducing myself. Sales textbooks will say that cold calling is inefficient. That's true, but since I did it during in-between time, if I picked up one or two good prospects each week, I was way ahead of where I'd be without these calls.

Finally, after my second week, management said it was time for me to go out on my own. No accounts. No leads. Just start out and see what happens. At this point, Bill Parke pulled me aside and delivered the sales training commencement address: "You can read all you want, study all you want, discuss and go to classes, but it really all comes down to two things—miles driven and people seen." He made it sound so simple. How could I argue? "Just get out of here and into the field where everything happens."

As the years went by, what Bill said to me that day rang truer and truer. But it ran against the grain of "conventional wisdom." As more sales gurus appeared on the scene and more and more self-help books were written and sold, the training of salespeople became a business unto itself. Almost as if it didn't matter if anyone ever sold anything, as long as courses were passed and certificates were awarded. Bill Parke's "miles driven, people seen" speech was laughed at as old school and unsophisticated.

Well, I didn't learn to swim until I got in the water, and I couldn't ride a bike without falling a few times. Until a salesperson finds out what it's like in a real-life situation, they will never learn what to do and what can be done.

⅄

Just recently, one of our Backyard Broadcasting managers, Craig Hodgson, put it to me best. He said, "With my new hires I give them a couple of days of orientation but get them out as quickly as possible. The longer they stay inside and away from the street, the more they begin to become reserved and hesitant. They begin to come up with imaginary objections, think more about what they don't know, and develop a fear of being face-to-face with a prospect. We end up feeding the call-reluctance monster. So I work to get them going and out on the street right away." This is right, and it is courageous on the part of the manager. The obsession with inside schooling creates comfort, not only for the salesperson but also for management, too.

Once new hires do hit the streets, it is certain that a percentage of them will fall down and never get up. That's just real-world math. Keeping these new hires in the office studying, keeps it safe. No one fails. Including the manager. No one likes to face the fact he or she hired someone who couldn't or didn't cut it. As long as school is in session, everyone is protected.

In the James Bond movie *From Russia With Love*, the film's villain, Rosa Kleb, is being shown through the bad guy's training facility. As grenades are exploded and machine guns fire, her escort says, "I hope our training methods meet with your approval." Colonel Kleb replies, "Training is useful, but there is no substitute for experience." To this her escort quips, "I agree. We use live targets as well."

Lately, there has been more support for the old school methods. It could be that the prolonged and deep recession has brought about a new appreciation for performers, those who actually get things done versus those with just grades and schooling.

Rich Karlgaard wrote about this recently in *Forbes* magazine. According to Karlgaard, "Salespeople who make more calls will almost always outperform salespeople who make fewer calls." That may seem easy to accept, but Karlgaard cited the key reason: "Frequent callers put themselves on a faster learning curve. They discover more rapidly what works and what doesn't." It gets back to this. The more prospects a salesperson talks to, the faster the salesperson will learn what will sell and how to sell it. I was lucky. I had a general manager who knew this and had the guts to shove me out the door.

⅄

Over the years, I have often been asked by people I've worked with, "What is the difference between radio in a small market and a large market?" From what I have seen during a span of forty years and from forty thousand sales calls in all different market sizes, the fundamentals are the same. Radio stations work to attract audience and then sell the value of that audience to advertisers. On the client side, the business people in Philadelphia were much the same as those in Clearfield and Williamsport, working hard to make smart buying decisions in order to have the right mix of merchandise at the right price to attract customers and give good service to get repeat business. Sure, the volume in a major market may be larger as a function of the population base, and there may be a need for better inventory tracking and more sophisticated accounting to support the size of the business. For example, in State College, the major local record retailer had one store, four thousand square feet, and served a trading area population of about sixty thousand (including the college students). In Philadelphia, Sound Odyssey had eight stores throughout Pennsylvania and New Jersey—a trading area of five million people, competition from two local groups of similar size, plus the national chains. Day-to-day decision making and working with customers, however, is very much the same in markets of all sizes.

⋏

From the radio station side, at WIFI, I learned the difference between a sales staff and a sales organization. Certain discipline came from the programming and business management: the strict inventory control, attention to commercial sound and content, and tight credit policy. From sales management came a sharp focus on daily activity. Management tracked revenue by day (just as retailers do) and the calls each person made each day. In the morning, I had to give the sales manager a form with a written plan for the day. Before I went home at night, I turned in the form again describing the outcome of each call. The sales assistant kept up-to-date files on each account, including all correspondence, past orders, and written presentations.

⋏

I learned to deal with more competitors too. Philadelphia had six big AMs in 1978 that were still doing the bulk of the market revenue. There were twelve FMs (including WIFI). Then there was television. The three VHF stations, the affiliates of the three major TV networks ABC, CBS, and NBC were channels 3, 6, and 10 and were not directly competitive with WIFI, at least for the types of accounts I was calling on. My accounts were not of the size to be able to use the large television stations. Then there were three UHF stations, 17, 29, and 48, who certainly competed with WIFI, as these television stations with their sports, movies, and reruns had plenty of "radio priced" inventory available. Also, competition existed from two very solid, very strong city broadsheet newspapers with special suburban sections and local pages to offer, as well as a daily tabloid and several suburban weekly papers.

While I knew I wasn't selling in a vacuum, and the competition was always circling my prospects, I never knew whom I'd be up against on any given call. It was necessary to be prepared to position radio and WIFI against any and all other media. This is where understanding the prospect's business, the specifics of their target customer, and their objectives in concrete terms came into play. I had to be able to offer a comprehensive description of WIFI and the methods the station used to attract an audience. I also had to show how that audience matched the client's target and what kind of track record the station had for stimulating response. Documented client success stories were an essential component of each presentation. These are basics, but, in the intensely competitive environment of Philadelphia, the advertiser's business was won only by salespeople able to execute these basics with professional consistency. The hard work and concentration paid off. WIFI's audience rank was generally eighth to twelfth, but the station's revenue rank among radio stations in the market was sixth or seventh, with WIFI's share of Philadelphia radio revenue one and a half times its audience share.

One tactic that WIFI used sparingly was the Saturday sales day. The first time I saw the sales manager call for a Saturday workday I looked around the room to see what the reaction was of the veteran salespeople. No reaction at all. Everyone just showed up on Saturday morning at 8:00 and hit the streets by 9:30, just like any other day.

I got two orders that first Saturday I spent on the street. A third order came in a week later due to the in-person call I made on Saturday that I never would have "had the time for" otherwise. Management called only a few of these Saturday sales days during my time at WIFI, but I did it on my own a few times and always found it to be beneficial. Clients absent during the week and impossible to find were somehow miraculously in their offices on Saturdays, relatively relaxed and welcoming.

I also found this to be true on those other times of the year when "no one is around." Days like the Friday afternoon before Memorial Day or Labor Day, the morning after Christmas, and on New Year's Eve. I loved the reaction when I walked into a car dealership one Saturday morning around 10:30, "What are you doing here?"

The fact these business owners were working and saw me working, too, created an immediate bond. Moreover, since these clients were not seeing other salespeople, I got some quality time I wouldn't have otherwise.

I remember taking the train up to Newark, New Jersey, for an 8:00 a.m. call on Bamberger's Department Store on December 26. The ad manager at Bamberger's was buying a special promotion on WIFI and paying for it with Whirlpool vendor money. The Whirlpool rep was there for the meeting (vendors always come when the retailer calls) and there to sign all the paperwork. The vendor was leaving for a family ski vacation that day, so we worked and had all the details wrapped up and the order booked by 10:00 a.m. Not a bad way to kick off a "dead week."

Most decision makers, being type A personalities, would rather be on the job than sitting around the house anyway, and they have a desire to be productive. Reviewing a proposal and acting on it gave these clients the opportunity to feel good about getting something done.

ᛉ

Although business at WIFI was always in a transactional mode with national and local agencies, we paid more than just lip service to the idea of penetration, meaning penetrating the agency above the media department level. And it was expected we know the clients, too.

John Tenaglia had a distinctive way of motivating people, but by paying attention to what John was saying, as opposed to his style of delivery, I learned a lot from him.

One of John's favorite moves was to stroll through the sales office late in the afternoon and eavesdrop on our phone calls. When John noticed a high degree of happy chitchat with agency media buyers, he would stop in the middle of the floor and shout, "Sellers who can't sell. Calling on buyers who can't buy." John Tenaglia made us think about how we were spending our time.

It was during this period that I was first told by a prospect that I should be looking seriously for a new line of work. Jack Pearson and his brother owned Pearson's Sporting Goods, and I proposed a campaign for the back-to-school selling season. The presentation was complete with all the pertinent data and a fully produced commercial to kick off the campaign. At the end of the demonstration, Jack said, "I'm going to do this, but I think it may be the last time we do business." (This was the first, and I think only time, I was bought and cancelled on the same call.) He went on, "You know you should be looking to move on as well. It seems to me the days when a radio station can attract an audience of any meaningful size are passing us by." Then Jack slowly, and almost sadly, finished, "They're going to put cassette tape decks in cars now."

All this man wanted to do was help me out. Literally, help me out of the business and on to a brighter future. I believe Jack was sincere. I don't think this was posturing, because he bought the plan I presented and went on to do business with me again. I just had to convince this client we were still on the air, and in spite of tape decks, radio and WIFI-92 still had an audience who would buy at Pearson's. Today when I hear about iPods, online music streams, and satellite channels and the fear of radio's demise, I always think of this sales call from 1979.

CHAPTER 18

THE ADVERTISING AGENCY

A s my one-year anniversary at WIFI drew near, management gave me some small advertising agencies to call on. This was thought to be a promotion for me. Most salespeople wanted agencies on their account lists so that when the agency landed business and put the account on radio, orders would come in. In other words, the agency would do the selling. The radio person would then pitch the agency for buys. After gaining experience working with media buyers at these smaller shops, I was assigned two of the top billing agencies in the city. As I was trained to do, I called regularly on the media buyers but made it a point to "penetrate" at least up to the level of media director. Over a period of several months, I was successful at getting to know Chet Harrington, the media director at Lewis and Gillman. One day, after having lunch together, Chet asked if there was anything he could do for me. I said yes and asked Chet to set up a meeting with the agency's account executives. I wanted to come in and present WIFI's upcoming program, Bridal Fair.

Bridal Fair was a nationally syndicated expo targeted at young brides-to-be and their mothers. The show ran in 100 markets across the country, and in each market, Bridal Fair chose the radio station with the best and most compatible audience to be the show's host. The station would arrange for a venue, usually a hotel ballroom or meeting center, and be responsible for selling all the booth space to local advertisers. The show normally ran in February, right after the football season, and in plenty of time to sell goods for spring weddings.

WIFI had just been chosen as Philadelphia's Bridal Fair station over WFIL who had the franchise for years. It was a real coup for WIFI, and I wanted to make the presentation, not only to put some of the agency's accounts in the program, but also to make a statement as to how WIFI had grown in stature. Chet was happy to help me. Two weeks later, I went to Lewis and Gillman with the Bridal Fair slide show under my arm. This was a first-class presentation on the "primary market"—those consumers starting out on a life of their own, buying their first table, chair, house, apartment, washer, dryer, life insurance. The presentation offered details on the "primary market" spending power and the lucrative opportunity for advertisers to capture this group.

I had seen the slide show at least a dozen times and had presented the show myself on a number of calls. In preparation for this meeting, I wrote, rehearsed, and then memorized my remarks. This was going to be fun.

When I got to the conference room, I discovered that my slide carousel didn't fit on the agency's machine. Not to worry, I was there in plenty of time. All I had to do was take each slide out of my wheel and fit it into the slot on their wheel. As I was finishing the slide transfer, the agency folks started filing in: the media director, two media planners, and three account executives. These were the agency's upper level people I wanted to impress. Four members of the media buying staff were there as well. (The four buyers resented having to give up their time to attend and weren't too happy with me going over their heads either.) My sales manager was along, and he sat in amazement that all those I claimed would be attending actually showed. When all were seated, I made a short opening statement and started the slide show, with all of my slides transferred to the agency's machine, but UPSIDE DOWN!

The expression of amazement on my manager's face turned to one of pain. Chet Harrington looked down at his notebook to avoid having eye contact with me or anyone else. The four buyers sat looking smug. So much for impressing the higher-ups. Now it was about survival. The best I could do was turn off the projector and go on with my talking points. Luckily, from experience, I knew the material in the show and was able to talk through much of it even without the slides, but this was hardly the optimal situation. Finally, I wrapped up and asked if anyone had any questions. One of the account executives spoke up, "This isn't really a question, but more of a comment. I had the same trouble with my slides a while back and came up with the idea of marking them in the upper left corner with a red dot so that I'd always know which end was up. That's worked really well for me."

I just nodded in thanks, not knowing whether to laugh or cry or jump through one of their fifteenth-story windows. It wasn't as if there was a lightning strike or a citywide blackout or even an unannounced fire drill. The slide show disaster was all mine. It was my fault entirely. I had some serious credibility rebuilding to do. This turned out to be a great example of what Nietzsche, Kelly Clarkson, or someone once said about what doesn't kill me. The challenge of regaining trust at Lewis and Gillman forced me to be stronger.

Assessing my status and realizing that good relations at the agency were essential to my income, I had to come up with better reasons to gain appointments and face time in the agency. It meant doing more homework about their clients, their clients' competitors, and any potential clients. I was physically in the agency offices at least once a week, consistently delivering research material and market information, not just selling points for my station but any kind of data I could find that looked as if it might help the agency people with their business.

Since agencies operate at the whims of their clients, agency personnel often find themselves in crisis mode. That meant there would be many opportunities for me to be of help.

A client waiting until the last minute to approve budgets drives the media department nuts. The buyers are forced to make a choice between waiting to place schedules, thereby losing leverage with the media, or buying ahead and then having to revise as the budget is finalized.

Creative may have to be changed on a moment's notice, meaning not only overtime for production, but also scrambling to communicate to the media to avoid the airing of wrong or dated copy. Then there's the personal stuff. I'd get a call from the buyer, "Hi, Pamela, what can I do for you?" "Barry," Pam would start, "*Chorus Line* is coming to Philadelphia next week, and my client must have four center orchestra seats. You do want our client to be happy with you, don't you?"

Therefore, whether it was obtaining impossible-to-get tickets, helping to re-arrange commercial schedules at the last minute, or delivering quality research, I made it my mission to serve superbly. As the weeks went by, the damage suffered in the conference room began to be repaired. My performance at the Bridal Fair presentation was either forgotten or excused. I went on to do sizeable business with Lewis and Gillman for the next four and a half years. What I saw repeatedly over my forty thousand calls is clients are always looking for good suppliers. So even when a salesperson has a day that is not 100 percent on the mark, if the salesperson perseveres and shows they are sincerely out to help, a client will meet a salesperson at least halfway. When the situation seems doomed, regroup and give it another shot.

CHAPTER 19

It's Business?

There was the franchisee of a midlevel fast food chain who was a regular and steady advertiser. One day, the client brought me into his office, closed the door, and said he was sorry but was giving my budget to another station. "I'm just not seeing the results I want," the franchisee said, "and maybe it's just time for a change." I went through all the usual phases a salesperson goes through when they hear bad news: disbelief, denial, anger, hatred, self-pity. I went through it all in about thirty seconds.

By the time I got back to my car, reality sunk in. It was my fault. The restaurant had been running commercials made available by the chain's corporate office. The commercials were well done by production value standards, but they lacked the call to action and urgency that I knew was needed to drive traffic and sales. Now the client was unhappy. The client blamed my station and/or me—same thing. He was right. I had been taking the orders, taking the money, and not holding myself accountable for getting results. At least, if I had been asking the client all along how we were performing for him, he might have expressed his dissatisfaction earlier, and maybe I would have come up with something different. Yet, I kept silent, kept pocketing the commissions. Now I was going to pay the price. I really couldn't stay angry with my client. He deserved more for the money he was investing with me—more attention to the results the restaurant was (or in this case wasn't) achieving. I realized two things that day: one, the clients pay the salespeople. The client may write the checks out to the station call letters or the big corporation in the sky, but the client is really sending the money to the salesperson. This is true in all transactions, but especially in advertising and radio in particular. Unlike when I was working at McDonald's or the men's store, where the customers would walk away with a hamburger or a new jacket. There was some trust involved, that the jacket's seams wouldn't come apart or the pickles were on the bun, but with advertising, as with other professions, legal and medical services come to mind, the goods the customer buys are not received immediately. The return on investment the advertiser desires comes somewhere down the road. There has to be, therefore, a very high degree of trust.

And that brings me to number two: business is all personal. Yes, I have heard the sales training tapes say, "Don't take things personally." I don't buy it. The client's decision to trust and pay the salesperson for their help and direction is personal. When the client chooses to discontinue doing business, or decides to take their business to someone else, the client may come up with all sorts of data-driven excuses, but in the end, it's personal. I took everything personally. Therefore, I had to take responsibility now. No one to blame but me for losing this business. It hurt when I heard the restaurant's commercials running on another station, but I felt the commercials from the corporate chain's home office wouldn't be delivering any better on this new station than they did on mine. I knew it would only be a short time before I had another chance. I decided to be proactive.

I noticed the restaurant continued to run coupon-like print ads once or twice a week in the daily newspaper. The ads always featured a specific item and a price offer. I remembered the client mentioning on occasion that he felt as if these ads in the paper got good response. (Here again, if I'd only been asking questions and listening for the answers all along.)

I met with one of our production guys back at the radio station, and we put together a great-sounding commercial that tied to the print ad. The next day, I went to see the franchisee and said, "Let me play something for you." I had the commercial on cassette ready to play three times back-to-back. Early into the second run, an expression of delight and joy appeared on the client's face. I will always remember how I felt while watching him. That marvelous feeling of knowing that what I was presenting was on target. By the time we finished listening to the commercial for the third time, my client couldn't contain himself. "That's absolutely terrific. Where did you get that? This is exactly what I've been telling corporate we need." The restaurant's radio advertising budget was back on my station, back with me. This was a breakthrough moment. I had finally woken up and given the client what he needed to make the restaurant's business better. It was too bad we had to go through the pain of a breakup, but it was fantastic having the business again.

⋏

One of my earliest lessons using this combination of persistence and taking business personally came as I walked in the front door of an army-navy store. It was early in the day, and as I walked in Jim, the owner, came rushing toward me. Thinking he was glad to see me, I gave him a big smile and hello, to which Jim barked, "I'm not buying any radio" as he pushed past me, stormed out the door, and walked down the street. Standing alone in the front of the store, feeling humiliated, I looked up at the two salespeople on the floor. I really couldn't tell what they were thinking. It was an odd moment and one that seemed to go on forever, even though it was just a few seconds. I had to try to talk to these guys. Maybe they'd tell me what I did wrong, because I sure couldn't figure it out. The three of us began making small talk, and then one of them said, "Don't worry about Jim. He's been pissed off for three days." I felt as if I might be getting somewhere, so I decided to hang in and probe. These guys might not tell me anything, but I had nothing to lose. "Why?" I asked. "What's wrong?" The one man looked at the other as if to get a sign it was OK to talk, then began, "Jim's pissed because the lease for our new store still isn't ready to sign, and it was supposed to be done a week ago." Not having any idea what he was talking about, I stayed silent and nodded, hoping he would continue. He did. "The new store is supposed to be open by the fifteenth of next month and that only gives us five weeks, and there's a bunch of stuff to do. You could really help us if you'd put together some cost estimates for the opening radio campaign. At least we'd have something to go by and could get a head start on that." Putting three and three together, I began to get the message that this little old army-navy store was about to quadruple in size with a brand new location, and it was all supposed to happen in about forty days.

I followed orders and went ahead, putting together scheduling recommendations. Then I had some creative recorded, just an open and a close, figuring I'd get merchandise details for the copy later on. With all this done, I set out trying to meet with the owner. I called Jim three times a day and stopped into the store every day for two weeks, Saturdays included, but I still couldn't pin him down. Jim was either not there, running between the store and the new location, at the lawyers' office, the bank, or in a meeting—secluded with one of his vendors—and could not be disturbed. Then one Friday night, I was wrapping up in the office at about a quarter till six and the station's afternoon personality ran into the sales office. "Hey man," he yelled. "There's some guy on line five who says he has to talk to you right away." It was Jim. I hopped in the car and sped to the store where the owner greeted me and hurriedly stated how (expletive deleted) everything was and how much he appreciated what I'd done for him. He said, "You kept calling me, and that's what I needed. With everything that's going on, you kept reminding me I had to get this advertising thing set up. Thank you for doing that and hanging in with me." Jim and I spent the next half hour going over the campaign ideas and getting the commercials and the schedule ready to go. I was thrilled when I heard this new and improved business come alive on the air. Hard to believe, just a few weeks earlier, the client almost knocked me over while he blew me off. I sure did take that personally. But the combination of taking business personally and being persistent helped me turn the situation into a positive, and, to this day, I smile every time I think about it.

CHAPTER 20

Cars

One of the reasons WIFI's share of Philadelphia radio revenue outperformed the station's audience share was the business WIFI did with auto dealers. The sales staff did a great job working the auto category. We didn't sit back and rely on dealer association buys from agencies but called on the dealers themselves, even the dealers who used advertising agencies. The sales staff employed dozens of tactics, but the foundation of the team's success was simple. When a salesperson claimed a car account, the salesperson made a commitment to see the dealer a minimum of once every week. Simple, not always easy. Yet critical. The car business moves too fast. Big changes can take place week to week. And as I was to find out, sometimes hour-by-hour.

In one instance, a Ford dealer who had not advertised with us looked to me to have strong potential. I started going into the store to see the dealer and was met with the usual reaction to initial calls on dealers—rejection. Nevertheless, I kept coming back. One week, I'd show new data on the car-buying consumer and that the Ford buyer matched up with WIFI's audience. The next week, I'd bring a sample commercial. Then, I'd show a testimonial from another dealer. I was rebuffed for a variety of reasons. The dealer would say, "We're doing all print." Then I'd see the store advertised on UHF television. On my next call, he would say, "We don't want your teenybopper station." Just one excuse after another. One thing I learned was that after about ten weeks prospects start repeating their list of excuses and, the second time through, the prospect and the excuses lose steam and the objections are less forceful.

One day, I went into the Ford store with a sample commercial for the dealership that I thought was particularly good and timely. When I walked in, the dealer saw me and my cassette deck and shouted, "NO. I don't want to hear anything. I don't want to see anything. Do not play that thing. Just come here." The dealer led me to a desk. We sat down, and he said, "Here's what I want. I want thirty commercials Tuesday through Saturday for the next four weeks. That's 120 commercials and here's what I want to talk about." He scribbled some notes on a pad, ripped off the sheet, and handed it to me. A quick glance told me the points were not far off from the commercial I had already prepared. However, I dare not mention that, much less try to play the commercial. We were on a roll. "Now, how much does that cost?" I presented the dealer with two prices based on two different distribution plans for the commercials. He picked the better plan but at the lower price. By this time I had learned most prospects, particularly car dealers, liked to do some negotiating over price, so I had already factored the wiggle room into my proposal. I didn't want to appear weak and cave too much, so I offered a price somewhere in between. He knocked that price down just a notch and I said, "Let's go!"

The campaign hit the air. I continued to come into the store to see the dealer every week, as always. At the start of the third week, everything was fine, everything on course. Two days later, when I was calling into the station, the sales assistant relayed the message that I was to cancel everything immediately. Not what I wanted to hear. Alarmed, I raced to the dealership. What could have gone wrong? Did I miss something? The dealer met with me and told me he was sorry, but we were done for now. That was it. No further discussion.

I reported this to Bill and Frank, my GM and sales manager, at the end of the day. I wanted to know, based on their extensive experience, what the two of them thought went wrong. My managers were totally nonplussed about the whole thing. I may as well have been telling them what kind of sandwich I had for lunch that day. The story of the dealer's cancellation seemed to mean nothing to them. They each shrugged and offered no advice or consolation. The next day, I stopped at the store, but the dealer was too busy to see me. I went back the next day. The dealer said, "Glad you're here. I need to start Saturday with seventy commercials for next week. What's the cost?" Unbelievable. I went from canceling forty-eight commercials to adding seventy in less than forty-eight hours. That's how fast everything changed. I told the story to my managers and again got no reaction. Bill and Frank had seen this movie many times. This is exactly why WIFI management insisted on the once-a-week call on all automotive accounts (and I learned that just once a week may not be enough). The attention paid to the dealers was how WIFI earned such a strong reputation and built such a strong business in the auto category. The station wasn't just running commercials, improving ups and selling cars, but possessed a spirit, an attitude. WIFI became known for understanding the car business: the necessity of being flexible and maintaining agility when working with the dealers.

WIFI had all sorts of procedures and policies by which the salespeople were required to live: copy deadlines, cancellation policies, advertiser commercials per daypart restrictions. All that went out the window when it came to the station's automotive customers. Only the beloved units/minutes per hour could not be touched. Management and ownership believed strongly in the infinite potential of the automotive category. Bill Parke would ask loudly in our sales meetings, "Who else but a car dealer can you see today and get a $10,000 order for this month?" Doing business with car dealers was fantastic—as long as you were willing to ride the roller coaster. The dealers were demanding and sometimes difficult. They were always surfing in unpredictable waves, and the WIFI sales staff was trained to acknowledge that and be willing to work through the up-and-down cycles of the day-to-day car business. For that, my fellow salespeople and I were handsomely rewarded.

CHAPTER 21

RECORDS

One day Bill Parke's car was being serviced, so he hitched a ride with the general manager of one of our competitors. This isn't as strange as it might sound. The two men lived in the same neighborhood, and the stations they managed were just two floors apart in the same office building. The competitor was in the AOR format, album oriented rock. While WIFI played only the hits, this AOR station played songs from albums that never made the Top40. The artists were all well known (The Who, Led Zeppelin, Pink Floyd) and most of the songs the station played were familiar. But AOR stations had a reputation for playing "deep cuts": one or two songs from each album that were not Top40 hits. This made AOR stations popular, particularly with men 18-34. So while this station was a competitor, their methods, and therefore their listeners, were different. Of course, some shared listening existed between the stations, but each station was distinct and had its own advertiser constituency. As I said before, WIFI was very strong with the auto dealers and that day, when these two friendly competitors got into the car, the AOR manager said to Bill, "If I hear one more car commercial on your station, I just might run us off the road." Bill's rival was envious and was always thinking that if his station had just a slice of WIFI's auto dollars, the additional revenue would be enough to make his bonus for the year. Laughing, our GM said, "Yeah, and if I hear one more record commercial on your station. . . ."

In 1979, record labels paid radio stations to run sixty-second commercials promoting new releases. The record executives believed it was a good investment to pay certain radio stations cash to air commercials with news of the product. Don't misunderstand. I am not talking about payola or any such thing. I am talking about commercials.

WIFI carried record advertising on the station, but it was limited because we played only hit singles. Singles sales were just a fraction of the lucrative album market, thus the bulk of a label's advertising budget would go to the album stations.

On one of my "ride around with the salesperson" days at WIFI, I got a master's degree on what the record industry really thinks about radio. We were calling on the representative from WEA (Warner, Elektra, Atlantic records). During this meeting, the record rep spoke freely about how important getting a record played on WIFI was to selling singles and establishing artists and, ultimately, in selling albums. He showed us how he tracked the number of plays on WIFI up against sales volume. His chart demonstrated the correlation. Getting a record played on WIFI-92 was money in the bank for a label. The record industry knows the value of radio. The whining from labels and artists about royalties is annoying.

It is now reported the NFL will be imposing a fee to the musical artists performing during the Super Bowl halftime show. The league feels entitled to payment in exchange for the showcase it provides. Should radio be taking notes?

CHAPTER 22

RATES

One last WIFI story; it is about the management of rates and commercial inventory. I spoke earlier about WIFI's self-imposed limitation of eight commercial minutes and twelve commercial units per hour. These limits were not universal among FM stations. Some stations ran a higher load but, with the intensity of the competition, all FM stations were held at a level necessary to maintain the audience. With these levels established and enforced by station management, advertisers became used to hearing that stations were "getting tight," i.e., commercial availabilities were scarce, sold out, or unable to clear the client's schedules. Some radio stations adopted TV-like selling customs. Advertisers would pay a higher price, a "bump rate," to preempt advertisers with lower-rate commercials. All of this worked well as long as the advertisers believed it when a station claimed to be sold out or nearly sold out. The advertisers only believe when the stations stick to their guns.

At WIFI, the salespeople never saw an avails report, a report generated by the business department showing how many commercials were sold and how many slots remained open in a given hour. This information was guarded by management. Management set the minimum acceptable rates. The salespeople had no ability to try to talk the sales manager into taking lower rates under the pretense of the station having unsold inventory. The sales manager had all the leverage. We had none. When it came to rates, we were powerless. Did management have to resort to games and gimmicks to cajole or motivate the sales staff to get better rates? No way. It was life and death. You got the rate, your order lived; if not, it died. Therefore, when a client pressed for rates below the minimum, the salesperson had no choice but to say no. That's right, turn down the business. This is what made us believable.

And that con game played by both buyers and sellers to drive rates down? No. WIFI never talked about "share of buy." This is when the buyer tells the salesperson that, in return for the station accepting lower rates, the agency will reward the station with a larger percentage of the dollars being placed. This supposedly gives the salesperson ammunition to convince the sales manager to take a lower price and gives the sales manager the ability to rationalize a concession.

The salespeople at WIFI couldn't play this game. We had no negotiating power against management. The rates were the rates.

And as Bill Parke always said, "How do you know you are getting a larger share? It's not as if we're going to be able to audit the books at the agency. The buyer can tell four stations they are all getting 40 percent of the buy."

I knew from talking with my peers at other stations that there were those who had more flexibility with their management. There are as many different ways of doing things as there are stations and managers. I was about to experience this first hand in my next career step.

CHAPTER 23

NATIONAL

I n the spring of 1980, I was recruited by the national rep firm Christal to be their Philadelphia manager. Radio and TV stations use national reps to sell for them outside the station's home market. The Philadelphia territory included all the agencies in Philadelphia, Pittsburgh, Baltimore, Washington, DC, and the state of Virginia. My job was to sell at the agencies in this territory for the Christal client stations located outside these markets. Stations looked at the national reps as extensions of the station's local sales staff. For example, I was the salesman for KTRH, Houston at agencies in my territory. Inside the territory, WWDC Washington's salespeople sold in Washington, but I sold for the station in Philadelphia. For WWSH, Philadelphia, the station's local staff did the selling in Philadelphia. In Pittsburgh, Baltimore, or Richmond, Virginia, however, I sold for WWSH.

The Christal Company had a long history in the business dating back to the 1950s. It was known as a quality firm due to its lineup of stations. Henry Christal, who founded the company, built the firm to represent stations with powerful signals and large coverage areas: stations such as WSB, Atlanta, KFI, Los Angeles, and KFAB, Omaha. By the time I arrived in 1980, Christal was owned by Cox Enterprises but was about to undertake a management buyout, led by the company president, Robert J. "Bob" Duffy. Bob was a young (just eleven years older than my twenty-nine), energetic, charismatic personality who led by example. Bob gave us three mantras by which to live:

Good selling is never wasted.

Pay attention to detail, leaving nothing to chance.

Make it happen.

"Good selling is never wasted." The sales call may result in an order, it may not, but never miss an opportunity to state the case, tell the story, and do it convincingly. A strong and solid selling call with an effective presentation is always the right use of time.

"Good selling is never wasted" kept the Christal sales team focused on the process rather than each outcome. In the national rep business, a salesperson is often handling dozens of transactions a day with countless ups and downs. Concentrating on the process kept the staff from riding too high or too low and kept us on the right path, performing the right tasks, in the proper way.

"Leave nothing to chance." Cover all the bases. Be sure to know and communicate the key selling points with everyone involved in the buying decision.

"Make it happen." Be proactive. Sell before there is a buy up. Presell your markets, your stations, yourself. The salesperson must create a desirable situation and put themselves in the best position to win. Take responsibility. Never blame anyone else for a loss. Never blame the station, the price, the buyer. Good selling means the salesperson puts the load on themselves and moves to the next step.

I loved being in the national rep business and working with stations and management of all types, in all parts of the country. In addition, my WIFI "the rates are the rates" training came in handy.

The station Christal represented in San Diego, KJQY, was owned by Heftel (the late Cecil Heftel) Broadcasting. It was a top-notch sales organization with a general sales manager who, while always pleasant, was also no nonsense. He held KJQY in esteem and stood fast by the station's rate card.

In the late 1970s and early 1980s, a national mass merchandiser, Best Products, dominated, before Wal-Mart expanded. Best Products used the Webb and Athey advertising agency in Richmond, Virginia. When it came time for me to present rates for Best Products for San Diego, the sales manager made it clear to me he knew his rates were going to be at the top end of the market, but he also said KJQY's inventory was in demand and would sell at these prices to someone. There was not going to be any discussion of lower rates. After the first round, Shirley, the agency buyer, let me know the rates were "too high" and needed to come down 5-10 percent, or she was going to pass on KJQY. I called the GSM immediately and told him this. He remained calm and quiet. "There's really nothing to talk about. I told you these were the rates and there is nothing to be said or done." I quickly pulled every bit of information available. I contacted Shirley at Webb and Athey, made my arguments with all the courage and enthusiasm I could muster, and pleaded a case for the rates we were charging. I wasn't at all sure how this was going to come down. First thing the next morning, we got our order. Excited, I called San Diego with the good news. "We got it," I squealed. Our GSM replied, "I knew you would." And maybe he did. Maybe the sales manager knew all that had to be said was no to the request for lower rates. Maybe he knew I'd take the challenge and do a better-than-average sales pitch to establish value. Maybe the sales manager knew the buyer would be impressed with the fact that we stuck by our rates. That KJQY had the conviction to be firm with the price. That we had such confidence in the station's position, and the position in the market was so strong and special that if she zipped us on the buy, someone else would buy those avails. And maybe that feeling, that feeling of missing something important, began to sink in. Maybe this buyer knew that showing her client at Best Products how cost efficient the buy was wouldn't be as impressive as showing her client a quality buy that included this dominant and prestigious station. I believe these thoughts and feelings exist and are present during every transaction. That every media buy is part logic and part emotion.

Remember, merchants are buyers. Merchants make decisions about buying merchandise every day and always with a mixture of logic and emotion. "Efficiency" is a factor, but only one factor. The store buyer wants what is right, what is good, what is going to make the store, the promotion, or the campaign a success.

An advertising agency buyer is the same, a mix of logic and emotion. Yes, the agency buyer has emotions, too, but may not put those true feelings on display. What the buyer shows on the outside is what that buyer wants the salesperson to see. What the buyer shows is a product of training and practice. Agency buyers are trained to keep salespeople at bay, make salespeople nervous, make salespeople feel small.

The agency buyer is a trained negotiator. The agency buyer learns to use every little trick, nuance, tone of voice, facial expression, and eye roll to posture for a better deal. It's what they do for a living. On my forty thousand calls, I have seen some real pros. One of my personal favorites, because she was so much fun to watch, was a buyer who would change the station on the radio in her office just before a salesperson came in. The buyer would switch the station to the salesperson's most direct competitor and, without saying a word, instantly put the salesperson back on their heels.

I saw for myself the value of sending gifts to agency buyer's offices: balloons, stuffed animals, basketballs, plaques, wall calendars with the station's logo and call letters clearly displayed. The buyers use them. They use them to subtly put off and put down salespeople from other stations.

A remarkable technique I saw used effectively was the pained expression. This is when a station salesperson walks in and the buyer pretends to be studying the latest ratings. The buyer barely looks up to make eye contact and then will sadly breathe, "Oh, ahh, it's too bad," and wearing a look of sorrow, the pained expression, convey sympathy to the salesperson regarding the station's latest ratings performance. "I'm so sorry to see what happened," she would sigh. It didn't matter how the station actually did. Since most salespeople were unprepared for this, the buyer was one up before the game even began. The salesperson was given no chance to gain position.

I came up with a way to negate this particular ploy. I called it "The Internal Memo," a one-sheet piece with very few numbers on it, but a brief narrative summarizing what took place in the most recent ratings report. The commentary was from the station's viewpoint and a concise rundown of how the station and its primary competitors performed, all honest and factual, but showing the station in the best possible light. The most important part of the piece was the headline, in extra boldface type:

CONFIDENTIAL
INTERNAL USE ONLY

When the salesperson placed this sheet in sight of an agency buyer, or any client, the buyer would first try to read it upside down, then have to use every ounce of self-control to keep from ripping the paper out of the salesperson's hands. After a few seconds, the salesperson would slowly turn the memo around and let the buyer see it and thus gain control of properly positioning the radio station.

⅄

National reps have always been accused of relying solely on numbers and being at the mercy of the ratings points. I recall a particular instance when I decided to forget the numbers entirely, and it solidified my belief that agency buyers are people too. Sometimes they're so buried in data, and if a salesperson will just tell a story, it can change everything. This happened during my first year at Christal while representing New York's country station, WHN-1050AM. WHN's audience shares were consistently in the 2.5-3.5 range among radio listeners twelve and older, and the station reliably ranked among the top-ten radio stations with listeners in the 25-54 age group, a respectable position that many stations would like to have. Over the years, WHN had built a strong agency business locally. The station's marketing to listeners, as well as to advertisers, was sharp, and their image was very positive. Nationally, however, problems prevailed. The biggest was, "Country? In New York? You must be joking." The bias against WHN was the emotional disconnect between the mental picture of country music and the perception of New York City. From the outside, New York is big buildings, massive crowds, shoving subway rides, graffiti, and crime. The city was a far cry from riding horseback on the ranch in Texas. The salespeople had reams of data showing WHN's audience strength in Northern New Jersey and Long Island, all part of the New York metro—but not part of the New York mental picture. The data was good, but the disconnect remained, "New York, Country, really?"

One day my head was hurting from all the banging against the wall I was doing trying to convince an agency buyer to put WHN on a packaged-goods food product buy for women 18-49. I decided to gamble and go in unarmed. When I strolled into the buyer's office with no briefcase, no folder, no computer runs, not even a notebook, the dynamic changed. I saw her physically adjust. She sat back, relaxing a bit. I pulled up a chair and we talked. We talked about the New York market, and its geographic, economic, and ethnic complexities. We talked about WHN, what role it played in the market and the relationship it fostered in certain pockets of that market. As we talked, with no numbers to squint at and no data to comprehend, the buyer began to feel and understand and appreciate where and how this station played a role. Country in New York. WHN was on the buy. The station was ecstatic. I was thrilled. And the buyer went on to become a successful broadcast executive (no kidding!).

$$\lambda$$

In November of 1982, Christal received word that the station we represented in Dallas had just been sold to a broadcast company that had its own in-house rep firm, thus we would no longer have that station to sell. No fault of ours, just one of those things, but still, Christal was now blank in Dallas, Texas. This would have a dramatically negative impact on our company's revenue.

It was a Sunday afternoon in New York, and the Christal executives and sales staff were about to wrap up the annual managers' retreat, forty-eight hours of intense meetings on the best way to sell ourselves, our client stations, and the markets served. Bob Duffy announced the solicitation team—comprised of himself, the company's research director, and the head of business development—was booked to fly to Dallas that evening. Presentations to prospective client stations were scheduled to begin the following morning. Then Bob delivered the commitment. "And," Bob stated, "we are not coming home until we have a new client." Thirty-two years later, and I still get goose bumps when I think of this moment. No fanfare, no happy talk, no call to arms, no "win one for the Gipper." Just a statement of the fact. Christal was not traveling to Dallas to have meetings, make friends, wine and dine, do nice stand-up presentations, although all of the above may be involved. The Christal team was going to Dallas to get a client and was not leaving until the mission was accomplished.

This was the most impactful lesson in leadership I have ever witnessed or experienced. Looking around the room, I could see and feel the lift in everyone's spirit. While there was no shame in losing our client the way we did, it was still a low point, a loss of momentum. That was all changed now. The course was determined, the plan revealed, and resolve made success a certainty. That's what "good selling" and "making it happen" are all about.

CHAPTER 24

TIME OUT

Special Report #3: Staying in Touch

"Stay in touch." How often do salespeople hear this? How often do salespeople do it? Do most salespeople even know how? When salespeople fail to close a sale, for whatever reason, the prospect normally extends the invitation to stay in touch. What does that really mean? How does a salesperson stay in touch and avoid crossing the line and becoming a pest? A nuisance? A time waster? And what is the difference between staying in touch and just hanging around? Many of my forty thousand sales calls were to stay in touch. When the prospect says to stay in touch, are they just trying to be nice, hoping in reality that the salesperson will leave and stay away, or does it mean the prospect wants to learn more and think about the proposal? The prospect may be very sincere about seeing the salesperson again. What I hear the prospect saying is, "Good-bye for now, but I'll see what you are really made of. I'll find out if the claims you make about the value of your product are true. If in fact you believe it yourself, you will stay in touch. You will be back. You will show me you care about me and my business. If you want my business, you'll be back."

This is where the sales process so often becomes bogged down and stalls.

Staying in touch takes time, effort, preparation, and a good dose of frequency. Staying in touch wouldn't be too tough if all a salesperson had to do was stop in to visit the prospect, or call to say hello. Real staying in touch goes beyond that, so it requires some thought.

In order to stay in touch, the salesperson is faced with coming up with a reason to see the prospect at least a couple times a month. Think about this from the prospect's point of view. What's going on that a salesperson can either show and tell about, or ask about, that is relevant right now to the prospect? Maybe the station just ran a campaign for one of its clients and a success story can be told, maybe the morning personality was just named "Best Of" in the market's popularity contest, the new ratings are better than ever, the station was given an award by the Rotary Club. Maybe the prospect is a travel agency, and a new hot destination was showcased in *Travel and Leisure* magazine that would be fantastic for the client to use as a commercial hook. What if the prospect is a retailer who just had a sale over the weekend, and now it's time to ask how it went, how many pairs of jeans were sold, and how the result compared to what the merchant was expecting? There are hundreds of topics to show and tell and ask about. Just think about what would be most interesting to the prospect.

As Dale Carnegie put it so well, "You can make more friends in two months by becoming interested in other people than you can in two years trying to get other people interested in you." Think about what's going on in the prospect's life and pick a good subject to use to stay in touch. Keep it specific. That's the way to avoid being a pest. Always have a topic. A salesperson may not hit the bull's-eye 100 percent of the time, but the prospect will appreciate the effort. Business people thirst for information. They know salespeople are out talking all day with people in the community, other business owners, and their competition. A salesperson's calls and visits will be welcome when the salesperson demonstrates having the interests of the client in mind and has the smarts to share relevant information.

I am reminded of the president of an advertising agency looking to make this point. He was sick and tired of salespeople showing up at his shop to say hello and literally waste his time. So the head of this agency marched down to his neighborhood sporting goods store, headed straight to the baseball/softball department, and purchased an actual base for field use. Back at the agency, he mounted it on the wall in the lobby. Underneath read the caption, "For those of you who have stopped in just to touch base. Be my guest."

PART THREE
THE RECENT OLD DAYS

CHAPTER 25

HEADING SOUTH

W**hen I left** Williamsport in 1977, Kerby Confer and Paul Rothfuss said, "Nice knowing you. Stay in touch."

So I did. Not every day, every week, or even every month, but when something would happen—sometimes personal, sometimes business—I would call. I called them when my wife and I had our first child. When I got a promotion or a new title, I'd be sure to call. Whenever they would buy or sell a station, I'd send congratulations. And if I learned of something going on in one of their markets or heard of an opportunity in another market that I thought would be of interest, I would make a point to send Kerby and Paul the information.

Staying in touch went on for five years, always by phone or through the mail. Then one day Kerby invited me to "come on down to Georgia" to get together in person. The three of us, Kerby, Paul, and I, met on a Sunday afternoon at Kerby's new home in Augusta, Georgia. We had dinner and talked through the night about what was going on in the radio industry and how their company had evolved. The company, Keymarket Communications, was in four markets now, all in the Southeast. We discussed what the next five years might bring for their company and my personal future. My desire was to get in on the ground floor of an emerging radio group where I could be a participant, not just an employee. I followed every move Keymarket was making and saw a good fit. We vowed, once again, to stay in touch.

Indeed we did. Two years later, I read in *Broadcasting Magazine* that Keymarket had filed an application to purchase a 50,000-watt Class B FM in Hammond, Louisiana. A little bit of homework showed that Hammond was the major city, population 20,000, in Tangipahoa Parish (what counties are called in Louisiana), population 120,000, and sat midway between Baton Rogue and New Orleans. My assessment was a Class B FM would provide solid coverage over the entire parish and about half of the two adjacent parishes and could be the dominant media player in the growing region to the northwest of New Orleans and the east of Baton Rouge. It looked to me to be an exciting possibility. I had been at Christal for four years now and was getting the itch to make another career leap.

I picked up the phone, called Kerby and Paul, told them I was ready to shift gears in my career and move to Hammond to be their general manager.

"Hammond?" they asked. "Why Hammond?" They were laughing. I told them I had looked things over and gave them my thoughts. "Do you know why we're buying Hammond?" I started in again on what I had already said, and they cut me off. "It's not Hammond, Barry," Kerby and Paul cried simultaneously. "It's Baton Rouge." The Hammond station, WTGI at 103.3, had applied for an upgrade to a 100,000-watt Class C1 and for an antenna move twenty miles to the west, giving the station city grade (70db) coverage over the Baton Rouge Metro. So in the span of about seven minutes, I went from wanting to be the general manager of a solid but small FM in Hammond to being the general manager of a brand new startup in a market of half a million people, Arbitron ranked number seventy-four.

I walked through the front door of our suburban Philadelphia house that night, kissed my wife, Karen, hello, had a family dinner, put the kids to bed, (we had a three-year-old and a nine-month-old), then sat on the sofa with Karen and said, "I talked with Kerby and Paul today, and we're moving to Baton Rouge." Karen matter-of-factly responded, "I'll call Dick in the morning." No, Dick wasn't a divorce lawyer. Dick was the realtor who sold us our house. Karen and I had thousands of hours of discussion over the past couple of years about our future and seizing this sort of opportunity. It wasn't a question of if, only when and where.

Six weeks later, March 15, 1984, Keymarket closed on the acquisition, and I moved into the Ramada Inn in Hammond. It was another two months before we sold our home in Philadelphia and closed on a new house in Baton Rouge. During those first weeks, I spent time at the station making sure everyone was working together and the revenue was coming in. I didn't want to have to dip into the company's credit line to fund operations.

Simultaneously, I began work on the new station for Baton Rouge. A 1,000-foot tower needed to be constructed, new studios and offices designed and built, and personnel and programming decisions made. It was a big project with thousands of details, and we had to move fast.

Speed was a factor because the FCC filings for the station's upgrade and antenna move were a matter of public record. The stations in Baton Rogue knew a new player was coming to town, and the less lead time they had to prepare for new competition the better. Also, the fall Arbitron ratings were scheduled to begin September 13, and we wanted to be on the air ahead of the start of the survey period.

The Baton Rogue market was healthy in 1984, and the media landscape was stable. The biggest player in town was family owned. The Manship family owned the newspaper, a VHF television station, a Class C FM doing full service AC/Top40, and the market's heritage AM station, which went on the air in 1934.

The advertisers had utmost regard for the Manship operation. I liked how strong, well respected, and high quality this group was and how their management was not shy about charging for it. The importance of having the leader in the market establishing rates and media value can't be overestimated.

Otherwise, in Baton Rouge, an insurance company owned the second-best FM facility and did CHR, as well as ran a VHF television station, and an independent owner of an FM did beautiful music, soon to be soft AC. Then there was privately owned WYNK, the station whose audience we decided to target, the country station.

We figured the country audience was being underserved, and WYNK had deficiencies to exploit. The WYNK signal was strong, the music good, and the personalities were OK. However, the station did very little in promotion and community involvement and played an enormous number of commercials: up to thirty units every hour. In a slow period, they'd run twenty. Overcommercialization left WYNK seriously vulnerable.

While work was progressing, it was still going to be a few months before the debut in Baton Rouge, and back in Hammond, it remained critical to maintain strong local revenue. It was also important for me to meet and get to know the station's top clients, as I wanted to retain as many of these as possible when the station moved.

My second week in Hammond, I got lucky. A charity dinner was being held at the gymnasium of Southeastern Louisiana University, right down the street from the radio station. One of the partners in the station's former ownership group still lived in Hammond, and he called me late in the afternoon on the day of the event and said he had an open seat at his table and asked if I wanted to go. I didn't think twice about saying yes.

A huge crowd was expected because the after dinner speaker was Governor Edwin Edwards. Always a character, Governor Edwards was known for his colorful quotes. When asked in 1983 about his chances for being elected, Edwards confidently stated, "The only way I lose this election is if I am caught in bed with a dead woman or a live boy."

Just before dinner was served, the giant doors at the far end of the gymnasium opened and in drove a Rolls Royce, the Governor's limo. Because of where our table was, and where my seat was, the Governor had to walk right by me to get to the steps going up to the dais. As he approached, I moved to get a better view, and, before I knew it, the Governor was right in front of me. I reflexively put out my hand to shake, and he did the same thing to the flashes of the cameras. My picture ended up in the Hammond Star, and the word was out there was a new kid in town.

The word was also out that this new kid was a "Yankee." I'll never know what people may have thought deep down, but I never felt my being a Yankee ever got in the way of doing business. In fact, I think, at first, it may have helped me get in the door. I got a sense that folks were curious to meet me and see in person the guy who had traveled more than 1,200 miles to work at their local radio station. One morning, I went to see a retail client, Sam, an older gentleman with a friendly, outgoing personality and a sense of humor. I could tell that Sam wanted to find out what sense of humor I had. He asked, "Son, do you know the difference between a Yankee and a damn Yankee?" "No sir," I admitted, "I'm afraid I don't." As the corners of Sam's mouth turned up, he slowly explained, "Well, son, a Yankee is somebody who comes down here and visits awhile and then goes home. A damn Yankee is somebody who comes down and decides they're going to stay." We laughed together and went about our business.

I certainly benefited from the geographical and cultural diversity of my forty thousand sales calls. I experienced firsthand that customers are customers. It doesn't matter if they are in Louisiana or Pennsylvania. The needs are the same.

During the six months Keymarket operated as a Hammond business, relationships in the community strengthened, and the station's revenue grew over prior year comparisons. The salespeople I inherited were dedicated, hardworking, and faithful in their sales duties. I provided the sales staff with some additional firepower in the way of sales promotions. The station involved clients to be registration points where listeners could go and sign up to win prizes, simple games that added excitement on the radio and gave the clients a way to see the drawing power of the station. We purchased a new production library to enhance the sound of the commercials. The salespeople took full advantage of these tools, bringing in new advertisers and increasing the expenditures from the station's existing clients.

CHAPTER 26

ASK

I hired Michael Baer as sales manager to work alongside me. Michael was born and raised in Arkansas and spent most of his career in Texas. In politics, they call this balancing the ticket. We were a good sales duo, but Michael was absolutely the best closer I had ever seen and have ever seen to this day.

In my sales experience, I never spent much time thinking about closing. To me it seemed as though closing was something that would naturally happen when the idea, the proposal, and the time were all right. What I didn't understand was that prospects like to be closed, and in fact, often need to be closed. Based on my forty thousand calls and watching Michael, I learned how important closing is to the prospect, the importance the prospect places on the salesperson asking for the order.

During one of our calls together, Michael was performing the art of closing with the owner of a carpet store who turned to me and said, "This guy is all right. He knows how to ask for business. You'd be sick if I told you how many people come in here and never ask. They're just wasting my time and theirs."

Prospects are seeing salespeople all day, listening to pitches and proposals constantly, about all sorts of things. Advertising, sure, but everything else, too, including merchandise, store décor, heating and air conditioning, storage space, and any new technological solutions that are available. Prospects tell me the overwhelming majority of salespeople fail to ask for the business. The salesperson makes the presentation. Some do a terrific job, but then pack up and leave. And most prospects, most of the time, will not close themselves. The prospect will not rifle through the salesperson's briefcase to find an order form to fill out.

When a salesperson convinces a prospect to take the time to hear a proposal, and then the salesperson leaves without asking for the order, the prospect actually takes offense. They feel cheated. The prospect feels the salesperson wasted their time. The prospect also feels the salesperson must not believe in what they are selling. If the salesperson believed, they would ask the prospect to believe as well. Failure to ask for the order kills any opportunity for future business. The prospect devoted time and attention to the presentation—the biggest buying sign a salesperson is ever going to get. To waste this interest leaves the prospect asking, "Why did I just sit and listen to this?"

Michael Baer didn't use closing tricks, or gimmicks, or the silly questions taught in many training sessions on closing. Michael, confidently and professionally, handed his pen to the prospect and put the order form or agreement in front of the prospect to sign, then would ask them to do so. Did every prospect sign every time? No, this is still the real world here. What did happen every time was the prospect would realize this wasn't an academic exercise. That if this prospect truly wanted to reach their stated objectives for their business, then action must be taken. That action may mean buying the station's proposal. It may mean the salesperson must now answer a thousand questions or do the entire presentation over again so that the prospect fully comprehends all the points. The salesperson may have to review the facts in order to connect all the dots for the prospect, or make adjustments in the proposal due to changes that have occurred since the previous call. Action may even mean an abandonment of the prospect's previously stated business objectives, a self-realization they do not have the wherewithal or stomach to move forward. No matter what, when a salesperson asks for the business, asks for the order, they are taken seriously, and when a salesperson is taken seriously and seen as a true professional with enough confidence in the product to ask for the order, that person will succeed in sales. The prospects will see to it. I learned from the best. Always do what a prospect wants. Ask for the order.

CHAPTER 27

PREPARE FOR LAUNCH

found a highly qualified engineer right there in Hammond. Wiley Traylor was experienced in radio and had worked at the public TV station. He was dabbling in new technology and computers. By hiring him, I may have kept Wiley from inventing Facebook, but he was intrigued and energized by the idea of building a new radio station. We worked very closely together that spring and summer. I was very fortunate to have him.

Also a new program director came my way, Russ Schell, who I had known from my Penn State days. Russ diligently put all the pieces of the programming and promotion plan together and had the station sound ready for prime time on sign-on day. We didn't like the concept of "get on the air and build as we go." With only one chance to make a first impression, we wanted to be at our best on day one.

We worked with Charlie Ochs as our program consultant. Charlie was a programming executive at Viacom who later furthered his career in top management with Infinity and CBS. Russ conferred with Charlie regularly on music programming, on-air talent selection, coaching of the talent, and promotional tactics. Charlie always told us exactly what he thought and was considerably blunt about it. Not always the best recipe for success as a consultant, but I loved Charlie's advice, and his style. His depth of experience in country radio really made a difference. Charlie helped Russ design a blend of music that turned out to be ideal for the Baton Rouge area and a style of on-air presentation that made us distinctive. His involvement sped up the preparation process and enabled us to have the station ready to go much faster than if we would have been left on our own.

The business manager, Veronica Fannaly, I retained from the prior ownership. She was smart and fun to work with—and did we ever have to work together. Managing the receivables/collections was a routine day in, day out effort. Managing the payables was something else. There was no corporate office on which to rely. Ronni and I sat down together at the start of each month and looked at the list. "Who must we pay first?" I would ask, making sure we took care of the essentials such as payroll, electricity, and rent. Then we'd look at which bills were most aged and consider who was calling us the most asking for payment. This was all an eye-opener for me. Here I was in the shoes of the customer, deciding what bills to pay and which of our vendors would have to wait. This was great experience for me and served as a good lesson for the sales staff. I was able to explain to them how their customers did the payables because I was doing it myself. I have never forgotten this and remained very sensitive to the challenges faced by our clients.

As a testament to the bonds we formed with the advertisers in Hammond, we threw a party for them just a few weeks prior to the format change from adult contemporary to country. At the party, we talked about the format change and played a thirty-minute sample of our new sound. The clients were very appreciative of being given this sneak preview and were supportive of the change, and most stayed with us. As time went on, our audience grew, and the station's rates became more expensive. It was impossible for the smaller clients to continue advertising on the station, but we always had a healthy representation of Hammond businesses.

Each day that summer, I started out with a visit to the tower site, arriving around 7:00 a.m. It's not that I had any actual work—I just wanted to ensure the tower crew showed up on time and in decent enough shape to work. Being only seventy-five minutes from the French Quarter, I imagined what the temptations were for half a dozen young guys away from home! Safety was my biggest concern, so my morning visits were intended to satisfy my own worries that all was in order. I was pleased we had no problems at all, even as we got toward the end of the project, and the crew worked over the last two weekends to get it finished.

I was not successful in getting on the air before the fall rating book began. The station was getting closer and closer to signing on, but it was just impossible for our engineer to be in more than one place at a time. He was constantly running from the studio to the transmitter site and losing hours of time each day driving back and forth.

Then a miracle happened. In the mail came a memo from Kerby and Paul about a relationship they had just formed with a consulting engineer out of Atlanta, Lynn Deppen. He had been a chief engineer in Buffalo and Tampa for Taft Broadcasting, and he knew the audio chain of a radio station inside and out. Lynn was now available to work for Keymarket stations by request. I called Lynn immediately and booked him on the next flight. He got to Baton Rouge late Thursday night, and we met at the tower site Friday at 7:00 a.m. I said, "Lynn, we are three days or three years from getting this station on the air. Do you think we can make it three days?" Lynn got to work with Wiley right away, and they had the station ready for a test that night. Just after 10:00 p.m. Friday night, Lynn and Wiley flipped two switches and suddenly 103.3 was blasting 100,000 watts into Baton Rouge. The technical facility performed as prescribed, and after a few minutes, we switched back to the original signal and power. Sign-on time for the new station was set for Sunday morning.

CHAPTER 28

BLAST OFF

A t 8:00 a.m. Sunday September 30, 1984, Willie Nelson sang "You Were Always on My Mind," and Baton Rouge had its new country station, Less Talk–More Music KAJUN-103FM, WKJN. Lynn went on to become the VP/engineering for Keymarket, and, to this day, I always say that without him I would still be wandering around in the woods in Louisiana, hoping to get on the air.

We had missed the first two and a half weeks of the fall book, so we launched our promotional campaign right away. The billboards were up by Tuesday. The TV started on Thursday night, and the direct mail dropped the following Monday.

When it came to administering our advertising budget, I borrowed an idea from a former contact. Donna Weber was the media director at Needham Harper, one of the agencies I had called on in Washington, DC, while at Christal. The agency was important to the Washington media because the agency handled the McDonald's account locally. She told me a story of a radio station that was changing format and had a significant budget to buy TV advertising. The station gave her and her agency the budget to place, so naturally, at the first opportunity, she bought a schedule for McDonald's on the radio station.

Being one of the largest local radio users, I knew McDonald's would be a big score for our new Baton Rouge station. I checked around and found that Gerald Garrison Advertising handled the McDonald's business in Baton Rouge. I went in and introduced myself and Gerald Garrison Advertising became the agency of record for the new WKJN. I had already planned what I wanted for our TV buy. The agency was thinking about points and efficiency. I wanted big shows. I didn't want the agency buying points and have us end up on *Phil Donohue* at 9:00 a.m. I stayed away from news, sports, and anything else where the content is unreliable. I made up a schedule using only prime time and the highest-rated shows each night: *Dallas*, *Dynasty*, and *Hill Street Blues*. The TV station people didn't like it. They wanted to sell broad rotators and put me in daytime. I knew, though, what WKJN needed. I wanted to reach the mobile audience, working people whose TV viewing is almost exclusively in the evening. I also wanted to impress the market's business people and embolden our sales team, "WKJN is advertising and spending big money. Shouldn't everybody?" The TV buy was more costly on a per-spot basis, but the reach was phenomenal and the quality of the programming surrounding the radio station's commercials sent our image with listeners and advertisers through the roof.

The impact was immediate. You could feel the excitement when we went live on location. The next week we hosted a night at Texas, the biggest country dance club in the region. The awareness of the station was already high. The entertainment that night was an up-and-comer, George Strait, and our special guest in the audience was Governor Edwards, who was a big country music fan. The Governor became a fan of our station, too. He would occasionally call our morning man to make requests.

⅄

While I was attending to the engineering, programming, advertising, and promotion, Michael Baer was busy recruiting salespeople, adding three new people to the team of three already in place.

Michael trained the staff to concentrate solely on direct business. That was where we knew our early success would be and how we wanted to build our base. If a salesperson made a contact that directed him or her to an agency, the salesperson had two choices: to continue to call on the account directly, or to turn the account over to the sales manager.

Baton Rouge had about a dozen agencies, and another dozen waited down the road in New Orleans; in all, these agencies were responsible for a good percentage of Baton Rouge radio dollars. The sales manager and I personally went to see the principals and the media department at each of these agencies. We made a complete presentation about WKJN, including its purpose and ways in which the station would serve the community. We showed them our rate card, although it was a grid rate card with about thirty-five different prices on it, intentionally designed to be confusing and unusable. Our aim was to retain the ability to devise custom rates for each client. We would then thank them for their time and make for the exits.

I know this is a total contradiction to my usual ask-for-the-business approach. Our idea was to play a little hard to get rather than starting out by begging for buys.

This also eliminated the standard agency pitch to clients of "We can get it for you cheaper." With WKJN, agencies couldn't get it cheaper, and we never allowed agencies to have house rates or cut bulk agency deals. Every account was dealt with individually, and the prices determined fairly.

The direct business started coming in right away. The direct clients always have a good sense for what's happening in the market. Local independent business people have to know what their customers are up to and how market tastes are changing or evolving. It's their livelihood. I saw this happen repeatedly over the years. Stations would make a move, be it an outright format flip or an adjustment of some kind, and the direct business would react weeks, and sometimes months, before the ratings would reflect any changes. In those first 120 days of WKJN, the station's revenue doubled each month.

"The clients are voting," we would cheer, "and we have a winner."

The ratings report released in January 1985 gave us confirmation. In our abbreviated fall book, (we not only missed the first two and a half weeks but also had no lead time to build an audience) WKJN pulled a 5.2 share of all radio listeners. Then in the spring report, released in August, we shot up to an 11.0 share, good for number two among all radio listeners twelve and older and a clear number one among adults in the 25-54 year-old age group. WKJN was firmly established as a leading Baton Rouge radio station, tops in the country format, and with the most desirable demographics. The direct clients were proven correct, and now, as the agency business started rolling in (McDonald's was first), the station dealt from a position of strength.

WKJN achieved success much faster than the original projections. Keymarket budgeted for the station to produce enough revenue in the first calendar year to break even. We exceeded the revenue goal by 50 percent and generated a healthy profit.

After the successful Baton Rouge launch of WKJN, we continued to market the station aggressively with television and outdoor advertising and on-air contesting, and maintained the limit of twelve commercial units per hour. The station was perceived as a quality product that produced results for clients. The team at WKJN was constantly praised for following up and for always coming through and doing what was promised to the clients. WKJN earned respect. I would often hear our clients voice their appreciation for our good work and attention to their needs.

One other factor in WKJN's rapid acceptance by advertisers was the sales staff never behaved defensively or negatively toward another station or another medium. Partly, this was due to WKJN being new—the outsider moving in. We felt going negative would not work for us. The sales staff was trained to make points, firmly, but the attitude was always positive.

In the presentation to prospects, the primary thrust was detailing how turning the WKJN audience into the client's customers would help the business achieve its objectives. When questioned about other radio stations or other media, the salespeople were always prepared to show the plusses and the minuses of each. "All advertising is good," the salespeople would say. "It just depends upon what you are trying to accomplish, who you want to reach, and what customers your business wants to recruit." The staff stayed on the offense creating momentum, which got the clients excited to hop on board. In the sales meetings, Michael would always say if a prospect turns us down it is only temporary. "We never lost a sale," the sales manager would cry. "Some just haven't been made yet."

CHAPTER 29

TIME OUT

Special Report #4: Programming

Having been away from the programming side for several years, it was personally enjoyable and gratifying to work with our staff on this project. The on-air performers at WKJN took tremendous pride in introducing this new radio station to the Baton Rouge area. They were dedicated to the market and delivering a service. The staff not only executed the basic format elements proficiently but also did so with a spirit that inspired an instant affinity with the listeners.

Whenever I think about programming, I think about two individuals: Norman Lear and William "Bill" Paley. Norman Lear was the creator, writer, and producer of *All in the Family*, *Sanford and Son*, *Maude*, and *One Day at a Time*. Bill Paley was the founder and longtime CEO of CBS.

Norman Lear comes to mind because he is the person I first heard credited with the phrase, "All hits are flukes." This quote appealed to me because it points to the fact that when programmers begin to analyze the relationship between creativity and ratings or financial success, they enter a world of the unknown. Research and analytics cannot be relied upon. When presenting a format or a show that is truly new, there is no certainty how the public will respond. When an artist with the track record of Norman Lear has the humility and common sense to say, "All hits are flukes," I pay attention.

Bill Paley ended up in broadcasting because his family owned a cigar business. They bought a radio station in 1927. The idea was to use the station to advertise the cigars. In less than a year, cigar sales doubled. Paley and his father said, "Hey, how about it? Radio works."

Paley went on to build the CBS radio network and then became a pioneer in television, always remembering that it's good programming, i.e., good content, that makes the business happen. The horse that pulls the cart is programming.

Paley had a special way of expressing his appreciation and understanding of programming:

"Programming is a certain gut instinct about what people will respond to, a kind of mystical connection between the broadcaster and his audience. If he has that instinct and can establish that connection, he can build an audience."

⅄

In Paley's day, it was Jack Benny, Milton Berle, and Burns and Allen in entertainment and Edward R. Morrow in news and information. Today it's Ryan, Steve Harvey, Rush and in the years just passed, Larry Lujack, The Real Don Steel, and Robert W. Morgan, along with countless others in local markets all across the country. Not creations of science, but warm humans with the "instinct" and the "mystical connection."

The other key to Bill Paley's success at CBS was his relationship with the performers, and his willingness to give them his time. The door to Paley's office at Black Rock was always open to his stars. He knew these talented individuals possessed special God-given skills. They were artists. Artists looking for his acceptance and tangible signs of his appreciation.

I always tried to remember to dole out chunks of time and remain accessible to the on-air people. It is important for them to be recognized for their role in the success enjoyed by the radio station.

This is not to discount details. I have always been fanatical about programming precision, where the breaks are and how long they should be, when and how often to air weather and other services, how the liners and station promos are positioned along with the proper use of jingles and recorded image material.

All of this must be mapped out and monitored vigilantly, as this, too, is part of making the connection. And when you've got it, you know it.

While driving around Baton Rouge one afternoon, I gazed through the windshield and looked out at the streets, the shops, the other cars, and the people, as if I were viewing a video, all while WKJN played through the speakers. It felt so right. I called a programming friend back in Pennsylvania to share my excitement as I proclaimed WKJN "The Soundtrack of the City."

A Harvard MBA from a bank once asked me what I do to assess a new market, and what I do to know when a station is on target even before any ratings information is available. I think my banker friend was expecting me to talk about some research study I use, but instead I told him the truth: I go to McDonald's. The banker squinted, as if to say, "You're putting me on." I said, "I go to McDonald's, buy a drink, sit in a booth, and watch the people. I may hear bits of their conversations, too, but mostly it's just to get a feel for the community and the market dynamics. While sitting there, I begin to hear in my head what would sound good as a backdrop." Maybe unorthodox, surely not scientific, but it works.

It works at least as well as chasing the ratings books. I tried to look at ratings as a report card and a guide but never as a definitive answer, and never as a predictor of the future. At best, the ratings are an "estimate," and Arbitron, now Nielsen Audio, is the first to remind subscribers these are only estimates.

About ten years ago, I was meeting with a few of the partners and analysts from a private equity firm that was interested in learning about the radio business. The firm had never made any investments in the industry but was considering it and was looking to get a better understanding of what makes a radio station succeed (or fail). In the three-hour meeting, I was peppered with questions about programming, sales, and capital expenditures. Then one of the analysts asked to see a ratings book. I pulled one off the shelf and watched as the group immediately went to the back of the book. They weren't looking to see any particular ratings. This was a general knowledge discussion. These investors wanted to examine the methodology, the sample size, take an especially close look at what is called standard deviation, the plus and minus factor of any given number. (A station with a six share may have a standard deviation of 1.5, which means the six is anywhere from a 4.5 to 7.5 share, obviously greatly affecting a station's rank in the market.) Remember, these weren't radio-advertising people I was meeting with. They were finance geeks, modeling wonks, numbers people. They studied the book for a few minutes and looked up at me. Finally, one of them asked, "And you guys go by this?" As statisticians, they were amazed at how rudimentary the process was and how susceptible it was to variation, what we in radio call wobbles.

Today there are two different methodologies from the same company: PPM (personal people meter) and diary. I get a kick out of the arguments about which is better, more reliable, or worse yet, accurate. Nielsen's stock answer is they are each right, and broadcasters go crazy over this. "They can't both be right," I hear. "I had a six when we were a diary market and now I have a two in PPM, so they can't both be right."

Of course, the methodologies aren't the same, but each is right subject to their limitations. When any kind of research survey uses two night and day different methodologies, it is likely there will be differing results. Putting a meter on a survey participant's belt to capture audio in PPM and asking survey respondents to chronicle their listening for a week in a diary are just different, not right and wrong.

Regardless of the research methodology, I avoided programming by the book. When you chase the book, you're programming from behind. As in the criticism of "leading from behind," you can't. It's an oxymoron. By definition, leadership means being ahead. And to be successful in making a connection with the listener, a station or personality must be looking to give the audience what they want, as, or before, they want it, not after the fact, when it is too late, and stale.

As Steve Jobs said repeatedly during the introductions of the iPod, iPhone, and iPad, "People don't know they want something that doesn't exist yet. You have to give it to them first."

Did the viewers tell the network they wanted *Seinfeld* before it arrived? No way, and it took a good while for the viewers to catch on. How about *Survivor*? Remember the first time that show aired? Would a research respondent ever have asked for *Survivor*?

How about Bruce Springsteen? Imagine how that preview would sound: "There is an artist, a singer/songwriter, but he has no singing voice and he plays rock but there is a blues and jazz influence to the music and the lyrics of the songs he writes deal with life in New Jersey."

Try getting a positive research response out of that!

Much discussion occurs about the ill effects PPM has had on programming now that broadcast executives can clearly see in the research when a station begins to drop listeners. Radio people, however, have been obsessed with what are called tune-out factors for the last thirty to thirty-five years. When a station devotes itself entirely to reducing negatives, it will eventually contract to a point where it is vulnerable to competition that has a similar lack of negatives. Reducing negatives is certainly a worthy objective, but with all the stations in a market working to eliminate negatives, only a station with positives will connect and attract new audience.

In the mid-1970s, when John Gehron programmed WLS in Chicago, the evening personality was John Landecker. Each night, Landecker would do his bit called Boogie Check—a series of clips of calls mostly from teens and young adults just yucking it up and saying silly things for fun on the radio. The bit was intended to run three minutes, replacing an entire song, and even this was considered long on this music radio station. Many nights the bit would run twice the intended length. In describing his feeling about this, Gehron said, "I cringe every time Boogie Check comes on knowing that we are seriously breaking format, violating listener expectations, and risking tune-out. Then I glow, knowing that Landecker is about to pick up a thousand new fans." This is leading. This is realizing that the elimination of tune-out will help you preserve the audience you have, but it always takes something else, something more, to grow the audience.

CHAPTER 30

TEXAS

In the summer of 1986, I took everything I learned from our customers in Baton Rouge and, along with my wife and our now six-year-old and three-year-old, piled into the Chevy and headed west on I-10 for 300 miles and my next assignment in Houston, Texas.

WKJN's owners, Keymarket Communications, had purchased three FMs from the Amaturo Group: KMJQ, Houston; KMJM, St. Louis; and WLTI, Detroit. I was sent to Houston as the general manager and, in addition, given the responsibility of oversight of the GMs in St. Louis and Detroit. All three stations were successful, but Houston represented about 80 percent of the value, so that's where I lived and spent most of my time. Once a week, or every other week, I'd fly up to St. Louis or Detroit, stay the night, and spend the next day with the team working at the stations and seeing clients.

KMJQ, MAJIC-102 in Houston was a giant. The station had gone through various phases since its sign-on in 1961, but MAJIC came on strong when it relaunched in 1978 as urban contemporary. MAJIC was Arbitron rated number one among all Houston radio listeners and was always the number two or three station in the Houston radio market's advertising revenue. The station was a model of performance and efficiency, known for profit margins approaching 50 percent, well above industry average. This station had it all. This was no start-up or turnaround, so what would there be for me to do?

Several weeks before we moved to Houston, my wife and I took a trip to the market to do some serious scouting around and arrange for a place to live. We sat in the coffee shop of the hotel waiting for the real estate agent to pick us up. We talked about the size of the station's operation and what a big business it was. My wife asked me, "Are you sure this is what you want?" I replied with no hesitation, "Yes, this is exactly what I want. This is like taking over as head coach of the Los Angeles Lakers." (The Lakers at that time were the Showtime Lakers of Magic Johnson and Kareem Abdul-Jabbar, the reigning NBA champions. If the Lakers won the championship, the coach got no credit. It's what everyone expected to happen. If the Lakers don't win it all, the coach is a bum and is shown the door.) "That is the ultimate challenge and exactly what I need." After the success we experienced with a start-up operation in Baton Rouge, I wanted all the pressure of delivering on expectations and leading an established number one station in a top-ten radio market of three million people.

July 1, 1986, I reported for my first day at KMJQ. We held a meeting of the entire staff so that I could introduce myself. After a few minutes about me, I turned the table and began to praise the staff for the success of the station and ask why they thought they were so good. The answer instantaneously came from all corners of the room. It was "The Block" they said.

The Block was a three-sided, ten-inch long, two-inch high, engraved wooden piece that each staff member had on his or her desk. Each side contained one word: *consistency, specificity, accountability.* Going around the room, the staff explained The Block was a constant reminder of how to conduct business.

Consistency: adhere to the tenants of the business and perform each task properly every time.

Specificity: know and communicate to each other exactly what is to be accomplished in detailed terms. No room for general bromides. Be exact.

Accountability: a two-way street, with staff members accountable to management and management accountable to staff with each taking ownership and responsibility for any and all action.

I loved The Block and Keymarket adopted the tool in each of its markets, eventually adding a fourth side, *follow-through.* Follow-through: circling back consistently to examine the work and evaluate for constant improvement.

As timing would have it, ten days after Keymarket closed the transaction and took over KMJQ, the spring ratings report came out, and MAJIC shares were down 15-20 percent across the board. At the same time, our morning man, Doc Kilgore, hired an agent and was threatening to quit. I ended up with a few things to do after all.

I told the morning man I was happy to work with him in a fair and even-handed manner, but in no way was I going to deal with his agent. Why would I open the door to that kind of relationship? The agent had already filled Doc's head with dreams of fame and fortune, so after meeting me, the morning man gave his notice. Before Doc was gone, I found an ideal replacement in Jim Snowden, who came in with a burst of energy and attitude and took the morning show to new heights.

Doc and I remained friends, and I hired him back two years later to do afternoons.

Meanwhile, I took a crash course in the black market, as radio users and consumers. I learned everything I could about the music the station played. The term *African-American* was not in the mainstream at that time. We referred to our format, our listeners, and our advertiser's customers as black. The community and staff were in sync with this.

After a few weeks, I was able to make some suggestions to Ron, our program director, which I knew would enhance our sound and hoped would restore the station's ratings. These recommendations changed how the station categorized the songs and improved the rotation system, allowing the biggest hits, as defined by the MAJIC audience, to play at a greater frequency and presenting the total playlist in a more consistent way to entice listeners to tune in more often and stay with the station for longer periods. Ron took the recommendations and executed perfectly. When the fall Arbitron rating book arrived in January 1987, the station had all its numbers back. When the winter book was published ninety days later, KMJQ's audience ratings in all age groups far surpassed any in the station's history.

With all of the station's success in the ratings, I expected revenue to be better than what I was seeing. The station's billing was barely ahead of the prior year and well behind the budgets Keymarket had forecast. National advertising dollars made up 25 percent of the station's business, and I knew there would be a lag time between ratings and dollars but, locally, it seemed business had softened up.

Part of this was due to local conditions. Houston, being an energy-dependent economy, was in the midst of a downturn in oil drilling. The ripple effect caused retail sales to slow and, therefore, radio revenue was off. The year Keymarket arrived in Houston, 1986, the radio advertising market was down 4 percent and headed for another minus 3 percent in 1987.

With market revenue down, rates and cost per points had declined as well. That is, advertisers and agencies were able to execute leverage and buy the same number of commercials or the same share of audience, points, for fewer dollars. This was not only due to radio stations fighting for the business, but television also encroached. On certain TV stations and certain time periods, the advertising rates were very close to what the top radio stations were charging. The only way for KMJQ to maintain revenue was to do a better job of inventory management. With MAJIC's limit of nine commercial units per hour, we had to sell the most desired days and time periods for higher unit rates while bringing additional advertisers to buy units going unsold in time periods in less demand. Studying the commercial avail report and revising the pricing became a daily activity.

There were other reasons for KMJQ's lackluster revenue. The number of salespeople was down. Several people left during the transition and either were not replaced or were replaced by unproven talent. But the biggest deterrent to the station's revenue growth was the general manager. That's right, me.

CHAPTER 31

Houston, We Have a Problem

While preoccupied with the programming revisions underway at KMJQ, and at the same time becoming acquainted with St. Louis and Detroit, I was not getting the job done with local sales in Houston. The improved ratings, plus a day I spent on calls in New York, put national on the upswing. Local was holding us back. Oh, I went to most of the sales meetings and was always on hand to make encouraging speeches. And I had been out with the salespeople and called on all the agencies. With most radio stations, this would've been enough. MAJIC was very different, as I was beginning to learn. While the quantity of listeners was never disputed, the station had real problems with the perceived quality of the audience. This perception was a major factor when it came to pricing. For example, if the market average cost per point was designated to be $110, KMJQ would usually be $135-140 based on our demand. The agencies would counter in the high $80s to low $90s, maybe, just maybe, agreeing that we might be worth $100. "After all . . . you're black." We didn't hear this just from the buyers in the media department. The perception ran rampant through the executive levels of the agencies as well.

Normal procedure calls for an agency to notify all the top stations in a marketplace when the agency is planning to purchase radio airtime for a client. The agency then takes proposals and rate quotes from the stations, and the buyer assembles what they believe to be the best lineup of stations in order to meet the criteria of the buy. The criteria state what depth of demographic reach and penetration the client desires and at what cost.

After the buy is prepared, it goes up the chain at the agency to the media supervisor, media director, and then to the account executive who presents the buy to the client for approval.

At this point, the agency account executive, who may also be a principal of the agency, is asking the client for the order, meaning the agency actually has approval to spend the client's money (the agency takes a percentage, usually 15 percent, of the media dollars being placed). The agency wants this meeting to go smoothly, with as few questions from the client as possible. The agency hopes there are no revisions that will delay the start of the campaign (and the generation of billing for the agency).

Customarily, the agency will show the client a list of the radio stations being purchased. What the agency fears most is the client will react to a set of call letters on the list, and it will hold up the entire process.

The client looks at the list and sees the call letters KDDD. Immediately the client shouts, "I hate that Robby Bozo in the morning. He's a flaming liberal and is bad for society."

The agency account executive is now held up, having to explain to the client how the agency buyer will rework things to eliminate the Bozo show or why the Bozo show is a great place to advertise. Either way, it stalls the process and puts the entire transaction in jeopardy.

When the list of Houston radio stations to be bought included KMJQ, the agency feared being in a position to have to defend buying a black radio station. Advertising agencies did not want to be held up attempting to articulate the value of the black consumer.

In the early days of KMJQ, before the station was established as a Houston market leader, agencies would routinely make buys and not notify MAJIC, a practice called "closeting." This allowed the agency to avoid the issue of dealing with their client about KMJQ during the approval process but caused another issue. Agencies sell advertisers on the fact that a business needs an agency because the agency provides unbiased, objective recommendations. Closeting any station conjures up the idea that the agency is starting the buying procedure with prejudice. For practical reasons, closeting ceased.

If in the beginning stages of putting a buy together, the agency buyer could deem KMJQ to be cost prohibitive, it would serve to eliminate the station and solve any problems that would potentially come up during the approval stage.

The buyer would tell our salesperson, "I am buying the radio market for $98.00 a point and you are coming in at $119.00. Unless you lower your rates, I am leaving you off the buy." This would precipitate a few rounds of back and forth between the salesperson and the buyer and often involve the station's sales manager too. In the end, even if KMJQ made some concessions and did offer a better price, the difference wouldn't be enough to reach the buyer's target number, and we would have to excuse ourselves from being on the buy, exactly what the agency wanted in the first place.

Another way the agencies dealt with their insecurity was to place a call to let the MAJIC salesperson know a buy was coming up (so we could never claim to be closeted) but that the call was merely a courtesy call, as KMJQ would not be considered.

"Hi, Joe, this is Amy from Gobble and Chew, and I'm getting ready to make a buy for our client Bill's FillUp, but they have a 'no black' dictate," i.e., the client, has instructed the agency not to buy black stations. The salesperson would reply, "Thank you so much for letting me know, Amy. I appreciate it. I can tell my sales manager. That way I won't get into trouble when we hear the commercials on other stations." Sometimes the salesperson would be stronger and reply, "This is really sad. Hopefully the client will change their mind someday so that we can do business." Then there might be some serious huffing and puffing around the station, under-the-breath cursing about how wrong this was, or a pity party in the sales manager's office, but it would end up with "that's how it is and what can we do about it anyway?"

With all due respect, this was a very difficult situation for the staff to deal with, and the salespeople at KMJQ did not know me that well yet. They didn't know how I might react if they told me of these difficulties. I just didn't hear about it at first. As I began to talk more with the salespeople, expressing my concerns regarding MAJIC's local sales productivity, and we talked about specific accounts, the problems came to light.

KMJQ had increased the number of salespeople, the ratings were fabulous, and I was convinced—based on what I was seeing—that the staff was working hard. All we had to do was deal with this bias and lack of understanding. I told the sales manager, Mary Ellen, to keep doing what she was doing, with one exception. Every day I wanted a report on any buy where MAJIC was omitted due to cost and anytime we were told there was a "no black" dictate.

To be fair, many advertisers knew the value of our audience, knew they had to have it. Some businesses even established special "black budgets." These were clients who super-served the black consumer and depended on KMJQ to deliver. MAJIC worked closely with these advertisers and their agencies.

We were being cut out of too many general market buys, and these were essential to KMJQ making revenue goals. The station could not afford to write off these agency buyers as being too hard to deal with, but also could not sell to them at a discount rate. As the reports came to me on problem clients, Mary Ellen and I decided to tackle them through the agencies. The station had a comprehensive easel presentation filled with documentation as to the size and significance of Houston's black consumer group. The market population was 20 percent black and represented a multibillion-dollar selling opportunity for the clients. The presentation was well designed, logical, factual, and compelling.

The sales manager and I began methodically trotting out the KMJQ presentation to the agencies, going up the organizational chart to at least the media director level. We were always given an audience and always politely received. I felt something was missing, however, when after multiple calls, nothing seemed to change. One day, while Mary Ellen and I were driving in the car after making a presentation, I commented to her how well done the presentation was. "Who put that together?" I asked. "Was it you?"

"No," she told me, "Kevin Sweeney did that."

Kevin Sweeney, a name I would hear again and again.

人

While working on the bias issue, we also had to contend with the Houston recession. The key to dealing with a downturn is to keep forging ahead and stay as close to normal operating routine as possible. The better management is able to produce a good product every day, promote the stations, and keep the staff functioning, the better equipped they'll be to rebound quickly when the tide turns. Being in the advertising sales business during a recession is extremely hard on the salespeople. It can really wear them down. Salespeople go out to convince clients they must continue to invest, and, at the same time, the station must be a good example. If stations cut services, reduce visibility, and trim staff, the clients will know it. In turn, it is what the clients will do. And they'll start by cutting the ad budget.

To help the sales staff maintain optimism, the focus must be on the process, not the result, while keeping a watchful eye on the quality of presentations and calls. At KMJQ, we came up with three mantras to get us through the tough time.

"Keep Moving."

"Do Good Work."

"Get Lucky!"

Keep moving, do good work, and get lucky. And if that's not enough, take the clients to Hong Kong.

CHAPTER 32

WORK THE PROBLEM

During my first six months at KMJQ, I was in regular communication with Joe Amaturo, the prior owner. As part of the transaction, The Amaturo Group, Inc. was owed the accounts receivable for the period up to the close, so Joe would check in from time to time on those collections. He was always interested in how MAJIC was doing and seemed impressed we were able to improve the ratings above the high benchmarks he had achieved. I think too, Joe took pride in how Keymarket kept the station involved in the community and paid close attention to our commitments to news and information. This was not so much to satisfy FCC requirements, as much of that regulation had been tossed aside by this time, but it was just good business. KMJQ's ratings success was only in part due to the music, personality, and promotion. Being recognized as a vital part of the black community was equally important.

One day, Joe and I had a lengthy conversation about what was called "The Big Trip." MAJIC had been doing these client trips for a number of years: to the Caribbean, Paris, Spain. The previous year, MAJIC took clients to San Francisco and Kauai. The trips were six-night excursions hosted by the general manager and, in this case, Joe, as well. All the planning and detail work was arranged by the station. The general manager hired a ground operator on site, but the airline, hotel, restaurants, and tours were all booked directly by the general manager. No travel agent involved. The idea was that this was the station's trip, and management was to be the true host, not just riding along with the clients on a trip put together by a third party. These trips were not sold to advertisers, as in "spend $x and get a trip." The clients invited would have to be at certain spending levels, but this went unspoken. The clients were invited personally to go on the trip, and the invitations were nontransferable. The station wanted only top-level people on The Big Trip. No advertising agency people, no third and fourth stringers. Only business owners, partners, officers, chief executives, perhaps a marketing officer, if senior enough. A Big Trip for the biggest players from the biggest clients. This way, everyone got along and could enjoy themselves. The guests were comfortable being among equals. While there were no formal business meetings during the trip, the entire trip was a business meeting. From the breakfasts in the morning to the cocktail hour in the station's suite in the evening, nearly everything discussed all day was business. This was a wonderful way for the station to deepen its relationships with its best customers and a way for the customers to develop friendships among themselves. How better for the president of a soft drink bottling company to spend quality time with the owner of a convenience store chain?

One of the elements of the Big Trip program was the post-trip party. Three or four months after the trip, the station would host a dinner for the guests. At the dinner, the station would make a brief announcement revealing the trip destination for the following year.

The reunion dinner for the clients who traveled to San Francisco and Kauai was scheduled for just a few weeks after Keymarket assumed ownership of KMJQ. I had no plan for the following year, and no announcement to make. Just before the party, the sales manager reminded me that the guests were going to be asking about what was coming up next and she asked what should be said. I whispered, "Don't make any commitments. It's just a thought, but ask what they think of Hong Kong." Where I got the idea of Hong Kong, I haven't a clue except that I liked the exotic sound of it. I was very sensitive about being the new guy here, and most of the clients coming to the party I had only met briefly, if at all. Joe Amaturo had owned the station for years and was trusted and respected by these clients. I knew people were asking each other and themselves about Keymarket. Would it be up to the task of running this premier property?

Would the new management be able to execute a first-class venture like the Big Trip? And me? I was the kid from Baton Rouge. How would I stack up in the major leagues? So the sales manager quietly leaked Hong Kong that night. The unanimous reaction was, "WOW. These new guys must be serious."

We booked the Regent Hotel in Hong Kong for six nights, and since the flight home was so long and we needed a stopover, we added the Four Seasons in San Francisco for a seventh night. Singapore Airlines took care of getting us around the world, and The Big Trip was now BIGGER than ever.

Keymarket and KMJQ sure were keeping up appearances even though I was becoming more frustrated with the station's sales performance. The St. Louis and Detroit stations were humming along just fine, as was the rest of Keymarket, with radio revenue across the country growing at a 5-7 percent clip. In Houston, though, we had a problem and we had to do better.

By phone, I told Joe Amaturo all about the Hong Kong trip. He seemed taken aback a bit by what I was spending but complimented me on having the good instincts to create a memorable event in order to establish Keymarket's image. I began to discuss with Joe the station's revenue challenges, pointing out that it was especially painful seeing a downturn in spite of how well MAJIC was performing in the ratings. That's when Joe turned the phrase that will live forever in my head: "Don't sell the station. Sell the market."

"Isn't it the market that's the problem? Isn't it the softness of the Houston economy that is causing my difficulties? How do I solve the problem by selling the market?"

"No, Barry. I am not talking about the Houston market. There is a market of six hundred thousand blacks and you own it. Sell that market. You are presenting to agencies. They are politely listening but are not acting. Only when you present to the highest officers at the client level will the presentation be effective and lead to action. MAJIC-102 is the conduit. Your radio station is what provides the client with access to this market. You have the keys, and you are the only one with the keys. Now start acting like it. There is only one person who can show you the way from here: Kevin Sweeney."

CHAPTER 33

KEVIN SWEENEY

knew who Kevin Sweeney was and was familiar with some of his teachings from reading a series of booklets he had published several years earlier. As a graduate of the University of Southern California in the early 1940s, he worked for CBS in sales promotion and then went on to manage a station in LA and was the sales manager of the market's first independent television station. He joined the Radio Advertising Bureau in 1952 and advanced as the organization's second president in 1954.

After a few years touring the country and making calls on advertisers on behalf of RAB, Kevin Sweeney became a consultant working for clients such as entrepreneurs Gordon McLendon, and Don Burden, RKO General, the most innovative radio programming group in the 1960s, and emerging independent operators Edens Broadcasting and the Amaturo Group.

With some reservation, Joe Amaturo agreed to introduce me to Kevin Sweeney. The offer came with a warning that Kevin had curtailed his professional activities and was only working for a small number of clients, people he had known for years and people he liked and admired. It was not very likely, in Joe's opinion, that Kevin would want to take on a new project like me. A few weeks went by and finally I got word that Kevin Sweeney had agreed to see me. He would communicate with me directly as to when and where. I was told to be patient. Kevin would work me into his schedule.

After several get-acquainted sessions, where Kevin interrogated me, Mary Ellen, our sales manager, and Keymarket President, Kerby Confer, Kevin agreed to come to Houston—just to look around. He booked his own travel, hotel, and car and did his own style of market research. Kevin and I had no contact during this visit. A few days later, I received a thorough written analysis of market conditions, KMJQ's competitive situation—not just in radio but in all media—and a blueprint for moving forward. Kevin began to work with KMJQ in the spring of 1987. He came to Houston every month and spent three nights and three days with me, our sales manager, and our salespeople. We'd start with a quick breakfast at 6:30 a.m. and go nonstop until we wrapped up over dessert, always dessert and always chocolate, sometime after 10:00 p.m.

Kevin was a tireless worker, always probing and digging for more information, more details, more facts, greater insight. When it came to giving us time, his generosity was boundless. He always promised unlimited phone time on the days he was not in the market and always delivered on this promise. Before he introduced the sales department and me to the complexities and sophistication of his methods, he helped us simplify the objective. "There is just one problem to worry about," he would say, "local sales."

All areas of local selling were addressed: recruiting, hiring, training, compensation plans, keeping good records on activity and files on the accounts, executing sales promotions, writing quality presentations, producing effective commercials, and documenting the station's success for clients. At times, it seemed overwhelming, but again, Kevin Sweeney stayed true to the principle that there was only one problem. That philosophy kept me in line and functioning.

Early on, I wanted to talk with Kevin about the salespeople and our expectations regarding their activity. I had come up with a loose idea of outlining this like a box score: the number of contacts, number of calls, number of dollars asked for, and closing percentages. Kevin sat silently as I showed him my proposed chart. When I got to the line concerning number of face-to-face calls per week, I stopped and said, "Kevin, this is really serious. This is the heart of the matter. What should the number be? Should it be ten, as in approximately two per day, or should it be fifteen? Could I go to twenty? What do you say? What should my directive be for the number of face-to-face calls I want our salespeople to make each week?" Kevin remained silent. We sat there without a sound for at least two minutes. He looked at me the whole time. I dare not say another word. Then, as if against his own will, as if breaking a promise he had made to himself, he answered, "How about one?"

"One?" I reacted. "One? One? That's ridiculous. How can we begin to make our numbers if our salespeople are only making one call a week?"

Again there was silence, but just for a few seconds. Then Kevin dropped the bomb, "Because one is more than what they are doing now."

Begrudgingly, I came around to understanding his point. A flurry of activity occurred every day. Salespeople were always moving at a high rate of speed, lots of busywork. A good degree of face-to-face contact happened but almost all of it with B, C, and D-level players, the majority in the Ds. What the salespeople were attempting to sell was basic radio babble, "My number is bigger than the other station's number and look at the deal you're getting." Occasionally, a salesperson created a well-conceived, nicely written proposal, but even these were delivered to C and D-level people, so they ended up meaning no incremental revenue.

When Kevin Sweeney talked about one call, he meant one real sales call, a face-to-face meeting, by appointment, with an A-level decision maker to present a plan to improve their business by solving a problem or exploiting an opportunity. One call per week was the requirement, and, of course, even one turned out to be unattainable at first.

The staff and I kept at it and got a little bit better each month. At last, we began to see a light at the end of the tunnel, growth in local sales that was contrary to the conditions in the overall marketplace.

The time I spent one-on-one with Kevin was all about business. We'd have long discussions about a particular category and even specific businesses. He was a walking encyclopedia, well before the Internet and Google. He could not only name the CEOs of the major banks and retailers in the country off the top of his head but also give you their resume; he knew how each CEO came up in their particular business and their strengths and interests.

All of this was relevant to the task at hand, as Kevin was instilling in me the overall business knowledge that would come into play when I sat face-to-face with company heads. He worked to prepare me for personal interaction on upcoming appointments. My number one favorite sales call of all time occurred during this period.

There was a regional department store chain, Foley's, based in Houston, with stores primarily in Texas and Oklahoma. At the time, Foley's was bouncing from owner to owner as the department store industry was going through a period of consolidation. In the summer of 1987, Foley's was owned by the May Company.

Foley's was a big newspaper advertiser and used television as well. Radio was employed for vendor campaigns for makeup, such as Clinique, and the usual storewide sales events (Foley's One Day Sale!) that seemed to take place almost weekly. Radio advertising would uptick slightly during the back-to-school and Christmas seasons.

KMJQ was having difficulty with the people placing Foley's media. Foley's had its own in-house advertising department, a broadcast buying director, and a radio buyer. The radio buyer was complaining our rates and cost per point were too high.

Eventually the buyer's complaints began to manifest themselves with reductions in Foley's expenditures on MAJIC; first in the size of the orders, then the frequency of the orders, and then the salesperson on the account was handed the ultimatum "get your costs down and in line with the rest of the market, or else." Or else turned out to be KMJQ being zipped from the buys.

Our salesperson countered with a call to the broadcast director. Our sales manager even spoke to the head of the advertising department, all to no avail. The message was the same, "Lower your prices, meet the market cost per point, or we'll take our business elsewhere." Foley's was an account too large for KMJQ to lose while the station was struggling to post overall revenue gains.

When Kevin came to town, he and I huddled and decided that a call must be made on the president of the chain, Michael Steinberg. I started working right away to get the appointment. Kevin and I spent countless hours on this topic. We talked about the store's current ownership and how Foley's fit into the May Company and what the future might bring. The president's track record and background were reviewed extensively. During lunch breaks, Kevin and I would hop in the car and visit a couple of stores just to walk around and get a feel for the direction of the chain's merchandising decisions.

All the while, I kept calling Steinberg's office to set up an appointment. His secretary was very professional and very kind, and, eventually, a date and time was arranged. Attending the meeting from the store would be the president, the VP/sales and promotion, the advertising manager, broadcast director and radio buyer.

The morning of the day the meeting was to be held I called the president's office to confirm. "Yes," his secretary said, "it's on the calendar. We'll see you at three o'clock."

A few minutes later, the secretary called me back. "We're so sorry, but Mr. Steinberg will be unable to attend your meeting," she reported. "The others will be there, so he said to go ahead without him." The moment of truth. I was playing in the big leagues now. They were throwing me a curve to find out if I really got game. Would I stand my ground or weaken? After months of working to get the meeting, would I take this consolation prize?

This is where Kevin Sweeney was invaluable. He had warned me something like this could happen, so I was disappointed, but not rattled.

"That's all right," I replied. "These things happen. We'll just reschedule." She gave me one more try. "The others will be there, so it will be fine to have the meeting today." My guess was her orders were to get this meeting off the president's docket.

I was firm. "If the four of them would like to meet with my sales manager, I will arrange that," I said. "But let's talk about rescheduling my meeting."

The meeting was reset for a week later. This time there were no last-minute ploys.

At 2:30 on the appointed Friday afternoon, I walked into Foley's executive offices. Seconds later the president appeared with his entourage. I was solo. And unarmed. No briefcase, no slide projector, no flip chart.

We walked into a small conference room. Michael Steinberg was a well-dressed, distinguished gentleman in his fifties. Although I was twenty years his junior, he was welcoming, and his gestures and tone of voice conveyed the utmost respect. I began to feel that my persistence and insistence in meeting with him and not allowing myself to be pushed to the B team had earned me a certain status. As we sat down at the table, the four employees lined up on one side, I on the other. The president sat down on my side with just an empty chair between us. *Interesting positioning*, I remember thinking.

While my message was for the president, I spoke to the entire group. Not using any material and not speaking from notes, I told the story and stated the facts. I explained the value of the black market in Houston and that KMJQ held the position of being the exclusive route to accessing this key consumer group. The radio station went to great lengths to create and maintain a quality product, and part of that was adhering to a predetermined number of commercials each hour. This discipline was intended to please our listeners and benefit our advertisers at the same time. Our prices were simply a by-product of the supply we had on hand and the fierce demand to reach the MAJIC audience. When I finished, the VP of sales and promotion spoke first. It was actually very good that she was part of the meeting. She was the person in charge of raising all the money. She was the one who worked the store's divisional merchandise managers and beat up the vendors to cut loose with the funds that created the money to buy all the advertising. She rebutted, "You just don't understand. Our media buyers have to be primarily concerned with cost per points. That's their job. Maybe your station is as good as you say, but you still have to get in line."

So we had finally reached the pivotal moment. "You know the story," I concluded. "You know all the facts. You know how imperative it is for you to invite my listeners to your stores. But if you are not interested, if you do not want my listeners as your customers, that is your decision, and I will not bother you anymore." Dead silence.

The president, ever so slightly, shook his head.

What does this mean? I asked myself. Was he about to argue? Dismiss the facts? Or just toss me out?

He spoke directly to his staff calmly, almost nonchalantly. "You put commercials on this man's radio station and you will see a volume of business we would otherwise never have."

What a climax.

As quickly as I could, while remaining natural, I made pleasantries with everyone, thanked the president for his hospitality, and walked out.

The whole situation turned around immediately. The Foley's orders returned to MAJIC at fair rates and everyone got along.

Michael Steinberg, the chief merchant, understood the inherent value in the KMJQ story and the importance of the black customer to Foley's. He was not at all bashful about it and clearly made his desire known to his advertising people.

⅄

I don't believe this call and the subsequent successful results could have occurred, as they occurred, without the training and coaching I received from Kevin Sweeney. Perhaps I would have gotten the appointment and attempted to be convincing, but there was an added air of confidence that came as a result of being so well prepared.

The salespeople and I went on to make dozens of these types of calls. While continuing to serve the agencies, we were now presenting the MAJIC story with a renewed sureness to bank presidents, heads of grocery chains, CEOs, and business owners. The dollars began to flow in. Within a few months, KMJQ was ranked number one among all stations for Houston radio local advertising revenue.

I learned during these calls that the "no black dictate" was usually fiction. The clients never said that. It was just something the agencies cooked up to get rid of us. As I talked with the clients to whom this statement was attributed, the dictate actually turned around. These clients were now instructing their agencies to buy KMJQ.

Kevin Sweeney and I continued to work together in various markets for the next ten years, until he passed away in 1997. I am grateful for the time I had with him and think about him every day.

A few years after his death, a colleague quizzed me about Kevin. Was the legend close to the truth? What about the stories of his training methods and insistence that you learn a magnitude of facts and do massive presentations?

I told him, "Kevin Sweeney boiled it down to two things: get face-to-face with the decision maker and tell the story of your success in specifics." That's it!

PART FOUR
THE MORE RECENT OLD DAYS

CHAPTER 34

GROUP RUNNER

The year 1989 arrived with big changes at Keymarket Communications. Paul Rothfuss left the company to buy a group of small-market radio stations. Some Keymarket markets and stations, including those in Houston, St. Louis, and Detroit were sold, and some traded, to bring the company to six stations in five markets: Austin, Charlotte, Columbia, SC, Harrisburg, and Memphis. Kerby moved me to corporate headquarters in Augusta, Georgia, and I was promoted to president and chief operating officer with responsibility of overseeing the day-to-day operations of the stations with the five market general managers reporting directly to me. Kerby held the office of chairman and chief executive officer, charting the company's overall course and scouting for additional stations to purchase.

Kerby's greatest strength was his ability to complement himself with those he put around him. He often said to me, "I wanted you as president, not because of our similarities, but because of our differences." Kerby gave me a unique pathway to realize my personal and professional goals. He still made the final decisions on buying and selling stations and the markets we chose. Though on the station operations level, he let me go, always giving support, and when I asked for it, guidance.

The promotion to president/COO was a wonderful opportunity for me. There was the stimulation of being a part of the fine team at corporate but also the enjoyment of going to the individual markets, working with our people, and helping them grow. I was on the road forty-four weeks a year, in the radio stations and on the streets. It was a great way for me to continue to build on the number of sales calls and client connections. I loved the variety of making sales calls in several different markets and being able to talk with the advertisers about what was going on in other markets that might be of interest. Seeing firsthand the impact and positive effects our stations were having on business for our clients strengthened my personal convictions of the power of radio, something I wouldn't get from just reading management reports. Proving, again, there is no substitute for being there.

$$\lambda$$

The Keymarket office had certainly grown quite a bit since the days I was doing payables with my business manager in Louisiana. Donald Alt had come in as chief financial officer with a staff of accountants, Lynn Deppen, the consulting engineer who had saved my life in Baton Rouge was now in-house and head of engineering, and our VP/programming was Frank Bell.

Frank and I had known each other for almost fifteen years, and I trusted him completely. We conferred on major moves like format changes or key personnel hires, but on the day-to-day programming, Frank was in charge. I encouraged our general managers to rely on Frank. The more they let Frank work with their program directors and drive the process, the better the stations were able to achieve my two objectives:

1. Stronger programming and ratings
2. A general manager whose time was devoted to sales

As the new president, I embarked on my first tour of the Keymarket stations and had a standard speech for general managers:

"The job is local sales. There will never be a lack of things to pull on your time, but rule number one for the general manager of a radio station is to take care of local sales and this is the case in Dallas as well as Duluth.

Keep the local sales momentum going forward. Use your time to work with sales management, the sales staff, prospects, and clients. This is not a secret to success, because this is no secret. Everyone knows this, but that doesn't mean it's easy to do.

Priority number one is local sales.

Remember this rule and you will always be on top of your game."

⅄

I did my best to be a good example. When working with the managers, I minimized any discussions of national, programming, and administrative topics. I knew the general managers sometimes found my obsession with local sales to be frustrating. I sensed they felt I was being unresponsive to other needs, but I knew if I gave in that I'd never be able to keep the focus on local. Rule number one helped the general managers keep their attention in the right place.

Having a dependable and talented ally in Frank Bell allowed me the luxury of using my time to implement local sales strategies with the stations and the general managers. As we worked through that first year together, our core team was functioning well, and it's a good thing because Keymarket Communications was about to grow dramatically; we began a furious flurry of activity that resulted in us closing the year 1989 with double the number of stations, twelve, in eight markets.

⅄

Keymarket's first acquisition in 1989 was WKRZ and its sister AM in Wilkes Barre, Pennsylvania. WKRZ was the number one station in the market and had been since its launch as a mass appeal Top40 in 1980. We paid a healthy multiple for it, about twelve times the station's 1988 operating income, but our plan was to grow WKRZ's cash flow to a level on par with Keymarket's existing station down the road in Harrisburg, WINK104. The big difference between the two was the revenue. WINK had about 50 percent more billing than WKRZ.

Again, the mission was simple. Grow local revenue. Rates and inventory had to be addressed. WKRZ had been running an excessive number of commercials, and so commercial rates were low. We also gave the station a more modern, brighter sound and a more active presence in the community. I recruited Gerald Getz, our sales manager in Harrisburg, to move north as the general manager.

No one understood the concept of "rule number one is local sales" better than Gerald. In fact, I may have learned it from him. Gerald walked into a difficult situation. Several of the larger local advertisers had bonded together to form an unofficial cartel. These clients felt that if they stuck together, all for one and one for all, they could hold the rates down. The station might be able to afford to lose one or two, the group calculated, but if each of these clients abandoned the station, WKRZ would be forced to cave. So in spite of the apparent improvements in the station's music, on-air personalities, and promotion, one by one these clients cancelled their advertising.

Gerald and I decided to let a little time pass to send the message we were not going to panic and drop our rates. Then we chose a small handful of clients to persuade. The station didn't have to convince everyone who had cancelled. We just needed two or three of them back, then the rest would follow along or be replaced.

I always love the mixture of logic and emotion that goes into business decisions, and I was about to see it firsthand as I personally went to see a few of the defectors. They were always happy getting attention from the president of the company. My taking the time to come to see them made these (former) clients feel important.

On the calls with these advertisers, I would let them know WKRZ viewed them as key clients and wanted to do business with them. Then I would explain that the station was not going to junk itself up with twenty commercials an hour any more. WKRZ would run a maximum of twelve commercial units per hour, and there was going to be room for only the finest businesses in the marketplace, not everyone. The business had a choice. Did the advertiser want to be among an elite group of clients on the best advertising medium in the market, or not?

The question was logical and emotional. WKRZ was going to give the clients what the clients really wanted. These advertisers never really wanted cheap rates; they just thought they did. What the businesses really wanted was effective advertising, good service, and a fair price. Exactly what WKRZ was going to provide.

Once a few clients were convinced and WKRZ stood by its commitment to quality radio and strong customer relations, the cartel fell apart. All but one or two members were back on the air on a regular basis. The experience of winning these businesses over increased the faith Gerald and I had in ourselves and in the WKRZ product.

If there was ever any doubt (and there wasn't) that Keymarket was headed for a huge success in the Wilkes Barre market, the following event convinced me for good.

I was in a sales meeting with the staff. One of the salespeople told us about a client she had seen that morning. She had presented the client a proposal for his store's clearance sale, along with a sample commercial. For some reason, the client was putting her off but was not voicing a specific objection. Our salesperson was tied up in knots, just stumped about what to do next. Gerald responded that in no uncertain terms the salesperson was to go back and tell the client, "Unless he commits to us now, the store may as well cancel the sale. There was no sense going to the trouble to plan this big sales event if the store was not going to promote it on WKRZ." I just smiled to myself, now that's confidence! Sales expert Zig Zeigler always said, "Sales is the transference of confidence from seller to buyer. When that takes place, a sale occurs."

Gerald's attitude and unwavering belief led him to build a terrific sales team, and the revenue goals Keymarket dreamt of were exceeded. With the new rate and inventory parameters in place, WKRZ had a group of core clients who felt like insiders, like season ticket holders. And there was a long line at the gate waiting to gain admission.

⅄

To increase the audience reach in Austin, Texas, Keymarket added an AM to the company's existing FM. This was another chapter in my continuing education on "combo selling." I say another chapter, as it was a reinforcement and reminder of what I had learned twelve years earlier as a salesman at WMAJ/WXLR.

The FM station in Austin KKMJ-MAJIC95 was a winner. One of the market's best facilities, a 100,000-watt Class C FM, the station was programmed adult contemporary. KKMJ's general manager, Johnny Andrews, had huge success with the FM he had previously managed in Phoenix, K-Lite, KKLT and used it as a model for KKMJ.

The sales staff was extremely good at positioning the station and selling the value of the low commercial load and quality audience.

Then the sales staff had the AM dumped in their laps and was told, "Sell this too." They couldn't, they didn't, and we all fought about it. Finally, to get management to shut up, the salespeople started bundling the AM with KKMJ, (bundle being code for giving it away) and this only hurt the value of the FM.

Just like years earlier in State College when I was on the sales staff. Try to force good salespeople with a successful station to add a completely nonassociated product (in the advertiser's eyes) and end up with disruption, confusion, and a devaluation of the main brand. Different market, different day, same story, I was embarrassed to admit. As the song asks, "When will we ever learn?"

⋏

Another project in the works was Richmond, Virginia. The station Keymarket bought wasn't in Richmond but licensed to Williamsburg, about fifty miles away. The idea was to apply to the FCC for a city of license change and immediately appreciate value by having a Richmond station.

Keymarket never executed this plan but sold the station during radio's consolidation in the 90s to a group who was able to move the station to Fort Lee, Virginia, only twenty-six miles from Richmond and close enough to be a factor in the market. We just operated the station for three years as a Williamsburg station and a Richmond pretender.

Under these circumstances, the staff in Virginia worked hard just to break even and keep the company from using corporate resources to fund operations. By the nature of the situation, the station had to run continuous sales promotions. This was a workshop of experimentation, and, when a promotion worked well, we introduced it in other markets. This incubator was a source of talent. Jim Kirkland, the program director, went on to play a major role in Keymarket.

⋏

Back in my old stompin' grounds of Louisiana, Kerby Confer and Donald Alt were in serious talks with the Jesuit priests at Loyola University in New Orleans. Loyola owned WWL-TV, WWL-AM, and WLMG-FM.

On the radio side, Loyola's cash flow had dropped to a point where the priests began to see that selling the stations and putting the proceeds in the bank would earn more in annual income and eliminate the risk and work of operating. When Loyola made the decision to sell and began entertaining offers, Keymarket submitted the winning bid.

It's always easy when looking back. Three years down the road, this purchase was a certified winner, ingenious, a steal. But looking at the state of affairs as we took over in August of 1989, I wouldn't have called this anything close to a sure thing. I was surprised the stations had any cash flow at all. Then I learned that all of the profits were generated by the all night truckers show, *The Road Gang*. WWL was a 50,000-watt clear channel AM. At that time, overnight drivers used it, along with WLW in Cincinnati and WBAP in Dallas, as their highway companion. A number of long-term advertising contracts made this a lucrative period. Outside of Midnight-5:00 a.m., WWL was running at a loss.

The FM market in New Orleans was dominated by two stations, WQUE and WYLD, catering to the market's large African-American population. The two stations sat number one and two, so the other dozen or so FMs competed for positions three and on. Our station, WLMG, was positioned as a soft adult contemporary with a 25-54 female target. Elsewhere, New Orleans had another FM adult contemporary WLTS, a CHR, WEZB, highly popular with adult females and a country station, WNOE. On a good day, WLMG was one of the pack.

Earlier that summer, I met with Johnny Andrews, our manager in Austin. I talked with him about the pending acquisition in New Orleans and that I wanted him to move there and run the operation. Johnny, his wife, and their two boys had only been in Austin for three years, and Johnny was becoming increasingly entrenched in the community. Austin is a hard place not to like, and Johnny and his family were loving it. The card I had to play was WWL. Johnny is a radioman through and through. He made his bones with Susquehanna Broadcasting, starting on-air in the 1960s. Radio is in his blood. The challenge of running WWL? Too exciting to pass up.

⋏

WWL-870AM went on the air in 1922. One of America's big radio stations, WWL could be heard at night in thirty-eight states. After enjoying years, decades, of wonderful prosperity, WWL, like many AM stations, had slipped.

By the mid-1980s, the station's audience shares among all radio listeners averaged in the 4s, occasionally dropping into the 3s. The station's audience had aged considerably, resulting in very poor performance with the advertisers' most desirable demographics. Revenue was hard to come by outside of the overnight *Road Gang* show, Saints football, and the carriage fees paid by LSU football. WWL was a recruiting aid for LSU. Since most of the games were played at night, parents knew that wherever they were in the Southeast, they could hear their sons play on WWL.

⅄

Keymarket viewed WWL as loaded with potential, but many skeptics existed in the market, both outside and inside the station. Just a few weeks before we took over, I was at the station talking with Eve Versteeg, the sales manager. Eve was always enthusiastic but was eager to know what to look forward to. She asked if I had any plans for WWL. "Yes, WWL will be the market's number one station," I told her. "You're so sure?" she asked. "Yes," I said, "I'm positive."

The staff had not been held accountable for years, so although there were good people on board, they didn't have the confidence to be winners. Johnny brought in a new program director, Bob Christopher, who was a breath of fresh air. Bob retained Diane Newman from the existing staff to be his right arm, and Diane was a big plus from the start. WWL took it one step at a time and most of the people stayed, played the game hard, and learned what it felt like to be on top.

⅄

When Keymarket decided to buy WWL, Frank Bell asked me, "What do you want to do about WWL? I never programmed a news talk station before."

"Neither have I," I said, "but don't worry about it. Call Ed Shane. He'll tell you what to do." Frank wrinkled his nose and said, "Ed Shane? The country guy?" "Yeah, that Ed Shane," I said. "He's great. You'll love him."

Shane Media was well known for its work with country stations. Ed's wife, Pam, was widely acclaimed as an expert country music analyst. Although they had worked with a variety of formats, Shane Media was always thought of first when it came to country. That reputation continues to this day, as Shane Media is the publisher of *Best in Texas* magazine, which follows the Texas music scene. What I knew about Ed Shane came from my experience with him back in 1983. At that time, I was still a national rep with Christal, and we were holding our annual management meeting in Houston. It was customary to invite the home market client to participate in these meetings, so our client, KTRH News Talk Radio 740AM, sent Ed Shane over to make a presentation. Ed was operating Shane Media at the time, but he was also in-house program director for KTRH.

Most of the news/talk programmers I knew were really news directors. The news stories and the presentation of those stories was how these program directors defined their jobs. Ed Shane couldn't have been more different. As he weaved through his presentation, explaining the subsets of the news/talk audience, how these listeners used the station, and what elements he had implemented to serve them, I sat in wonderment and thought, *This is really wild.* Here's a guy who is a program director, a radio program director taking all the experience, knowledge, and tactics from music radio, whether it be country, rock, AC, or Top40, and applying them to news/talk. I knew KTRH was humming. Now I knew why.

With Ed on board consulting WWL, we produced a plan to move the station into the twentieth century. Then, unexpectedly, Kerby called me and said, "Let's put Rush Limbaugh on WWL." "Rush what, who, why?" I asked. I wasn't too keen on the idea, because it was a network show and an unproven one at that. Who knew if it would even be around in a few months? I thought we needed a local New Orleans host on WWL in midday. Kerby liked the sound of the Limbaugh show, the use of a Top40 format structure for a talk show, and he thought Rush—unlike most of the talk show hosts in the late 80s—was entertaining, not just informative. It didn't take long for me to go along, especially since the current local WWL host had no energy and no ratings, and I didn't have a better solution.

The network was trying to make a go of it, so Rush Limbaugh was very excited about being picked up by WWL. This was a major accomplishment, and he was determined to see that it worked. Rush came to town several times for speaking engagements and to help us with advertisers. Being a big NFL football fan, Rush would come down from New York on Sundays and entertain clients with us in the suite before Saints games. So two of WWL's problems, low mid-day ratings and very little revenue in the time period, were solved. We now had a strong performer on-air, and, since Rush was so willing to work with us, it was like having a local personality. The move paid off for everyone; WWL had growing strength with audience ratings in midday and Rush was proving to the world that he could succeed doing a network show.

The Rush Limbaugh show was growing in affiliates every day, and through the early 1990s, Rush became a national figure. WWL's Johnny Andrews appeared on *60 Minutes* on CBS during a segment on the Rush phenomenon, and Rush was a cover story on *Time* and other magazines.

During this time, on a visit to New York, I stopped by to see Rush at the WABC studios. I got there about 2:45 p.m. and sat across the glass with his executive producer, "chief of all things," Kit Carson, for the last fifteen minutes of the program. At the conclusion of the broadcast, Rush motioned for me to come in. This was strictly a social call and we had a friendly chat for fifteen to twenty minutes. Rush was beaming with his widespread notoriety and marveled at how everyone was asking, "What is this Rush Limbaugh? Who is this man? What's it all about? What does it all mean?" To that Rush laughed and said, "It's just a good show."

I'll never forget that, and I don't think Rush Limbaugh has either. I just saw him at his twenty-fifth anniversary celebration at the Radio Show in Orlando. He spoke very warmly about his success to a small group of long-term affiliates. He voiced his appreciation and said how grateful he was to the stations. Rush told us of his early days in radio and his desire to be on the air on a big station. Rush said he understood then that you can only be a big star when you have a big stage.

⅄

All the pieces were in place: Ed Shane working with Frank Bell and Bob Christopher on the programming details, Johnny Andrews encouraging the team and allowing the talent to flourish, and to top it off, Rush Limbaugh. WWL was reborn and began showing audience ratings gains right away. By early 1991, the station was number one.

While WWL was being readied for liftoff, I continued to make the rounds covering all the Keymarket stations and was about to have some fun in Charlotte. We were still doing beautiful music on WRLX, the place to relax. This was the old-style easy listening music format playing instrumental versions of popular songs. And by instrumental, the dominant instrument being the violin. It was a tough way to make a living in 1989, as the station had no appeal to anyone under the age of 50.

EZ Communications, a well-run and highly respected group, owned WEZC in Charlotte and was programming soft adult contemporary. The station was a consistently strong performer, particularly with female listeners 35-54 years of age. WEZC decided there were bigger shares, better demographics, and more revenue potential in a hot AC format, so they made the move and changed their call letters to WMXC-The MIX104.7.

This left a big void in the Charlotte market and a big opportunity for Keymarket. The minute WEZC changed to the MIX, I called our attorney in Washington and had him run over to the FCC to grab the WEZC call letters for us. Frank Bell quickly tossed off the violins and updated the station's music to soft AC. Within a few days, there were billboards and newspaper ads with the message: WEZC Has Moved to 102.9. We followed up with a television campaign. This sleepy "elevator music" station was suddenly a ratings leader with women in the 25-54 age group. Of course, the revenue began to grow the minute we flipped to WEZC. The Charlotte advertisers caught on and were impressed with the ingenuity and speed of our move. When I was in the market seeing clients, I remember talking with Harry Bush, of Bush Stationers, who was a good radio user and always took pride in his understanding of the media. Harry was a client of ours in the beautiful music format but was thrilled with the format change. He said, "This is great. This gives me a better audience than I was getting with your old format, and I must tell you, I got a kick out of how you stole the thunder from EZ Communications. You guys are geniuses." "Harry, I'm not sure we're geniuses," I said. "We just know how to take yes for an answer." This one was really handed to us, and we made the most of it.

CHAPTER 35

GO WEST

The last big project of 1989 took place out west. Kerby Confer heard about an FM station in San Bernardino, KQLH, which was put in bankruptcy. The present owner was fighting to keep the station, and another local group was trying to get it. Keymarket entered the fray and, finally, the judge set a date to settle the matter.

Donald Alt took off for Southern California to appear in court and state our case, although Donald had a bit more ammunition than just his words. As the parties appeared before the judge and told their stories, Donald punctuated his by producing a check that he was willing to turn over to the court at that moment. The amount of the check would satisfy the creditors and solve the whole affair. The judge asked the other parties if they could do likewise. The two just hung their heads, and it was all over. Keymarket won! We had our 50,000-watt Class B FM covering Riverside-San Bernardino, California.

ᛉ

KQLH was doing adult contemporary, and we could have left the format in place, but Kerby wanted to do country. The logic was sound. In studying the performance of all the stations in the market, it was apparent there was a good appetite for country. The format was only being done by AM stations and a couple of small 3,000-watt Class A FMs in a style more appealing to older demographics.

No one station alone had the facility to cover the market. Adding up all the audience shares of these smaller stations produced a figure approaching twenty. We just figured with its superior signal and regional coverage, KQLH could capture half of that audience, and Keymarket would have a major triumph.

Once the decision was made to go country, Frank Bell called our friend and country expert, Ed Shane. Along with Pam, Ed came to town and studied the market. We closed the transaction on the station that fall and hustled to prepare for the format change. The music had to be selected and scheduled, new jingles ordered, a station voice chosen, and staff recruited. Not everyone on the KQLH staff wanted to make the move to country. In fact, many people in the market were negative about country. The conventional wisdom was that this is Southern California. Country doesn't play well here. The problem was there wasn't any history of country radio being strong. As I said, it was only on smaller stations and, once again, here we go asking potential listeners to evaluate something they don't already have. Predictive research is fraught with peril. The audience wouldn't know they wanted a contemporary country station until they heard it.

On Christmas Day 1989, Keymarket launched KFRG-95.1 "K-Frog, The Best and Most Country." The station took off like a rocket. Advertisers, knowing their customers, and what's happening in their market, began asking for annual agreements and bulk contracts. These smart business people figured that if they got in early, they would be grandfathered with better rates.

Borrowing a page from my Houston experience, I worked with the sales staff to develop a presentation to sell the market, not the station. In this case, the market story was a geographic story. Riverside-San Bernardino is a separate Arbitron metro for radio but is part of the Los Angeles television DMA. Thinking among the agencies in LA was that Riverside and San Bernardino consumers would be effectively delivered through the spillover from the client's LA buy. KFRG had to attack this claim. The KFRG presentation demonstrated the quality and buying power of the population in the Riverside-San Bernardino metro. Then, it went on to show how KFRG—with programming specifically targeted to the local market and regional news, community information, and promotions—would deliver that market so much better than leaving it to the LA stations, which had no real presence or concentration in our territory.

The Los Angeles agencies and buying services liked our story. It made total sense, and I think that the agencies used our presentation to get additional budget from their clients to cover the growing population in this important geography. Everybody was happy.

Everybody except Richard McIntosh, our general manager. He was happy enough receiving the orders and seeing the money rolling in, but for the first time in his life, he had to manage the inventory and it was difficult. KFRG was limited to twelve commercial units an hour, and with the rush on the station from local clients and the quick acceptance of our story from the LA shops, the demand was overwhelming. There was no way we were going to break KFRG's commercial format. Richard never asked about that. He was smart and knew that holding on, as wild a ride as it was, would pay off. He craftily moved the rates up and massaged bruised clients and buyers, putting KFRG on a solid course.

CHAPTER 36

HERE WE GO AGAIN

The Alan Greenspans, Ben Bernankes, and Janet Yellens of the world could make their lives a lot easier if, instead of spending time with politicians, bankers, and other Ivy League economists, they'd just visit radio stations. The most accurate barometer of the economy is the local advertiser. If talking with the local advertiser is not possible, then talk with a radio station business manager. Before anyone in Washington, DC, or New York screams recession, radio's accounts receivable will show the amounts in the 90-days+ and 120-days+ columns growing larger. Clients will begin to stretch out the time it takes for them to pay their bills.

During the first quarter of 1990, I began to hear from clients I considered reliable and trusted sources that consumers were holding back on spending. These weren't the usual sky-is-falling diversions that clients will sometimes employ to negotiate a better deal. These were solid reports from people I knew would give me the straight scoop. Bernie Siegel was one such contact. Bernie owned Bello Jewelers in Harrisburg. I would make a point to see Bernie during my trips to the market and was confident he would always relay honest and accurate intelligence on local business conditions. When he confided that sales were coming up short against his same-day numbers from the previous year, I knew I had better pay attention. As I started to get similar reports from other business owners in other markets and see our accounts receivable stretch out as clients delayed payments, it began to feel like Houston all over again. A full-scale national recession was on the way. The general managers and I reacted. I might say overreacted. My team devised more sales promotions, packages, and advertiser incentives. We must have presented three years' worth of specials from February through July of 1990.

In Pennsylvania, we hosted advertiser banquets with terrific prizes for clients to bid on. Participating clients were awarded funny money, the amount equal to what the client had invested with the station, to be used during the prize auction. The company took a group of advertisers from four of the markets to Bermuda. In New Orleans, WWL published a 98-page Louisiana weather almanac that included a foldout hurricane tracking map, filled with ads. WWL followed that up with the *Game Guide*, a preseason football publication in the summer. Not to be left behind, the FM, WLMG, published the *Expectant Mother's Guide*. Register-to-win contests were plentiful; clients who bought the programs became registration points in an effort to boost in-store traffic. Prizes ranged from stuffed panda dolls in "Panda-Monium" to giant stuffed Easter Bunnies to trips to Paris. In Austin, Texas, the stations put a planeload of agency people on a flight to New Orleans for a long weekend in the French Quarter. (I was told they all returned.)

We took the Bridal Fair idea and replicated it repeatedly. There were the Working Women's Expo, the Baby Fair, The Kids Fair, the Home and Garden Show, and the Big Boy Toy Show, a gadgets, sports gear, and electronics expo for men. If a station could sell booth space, it invented a show.

As the economy faltered, sales management knew business people were going to avoid spending money for anything until the wind direction changed. Convincing businesses to advertise was going to be tough, so the stations laid on as much other stuff as possible to encourage clients to invest with us.

Of course, when the Iraqis invaded Kuwait in August of 1990, it set the stage for the first down year for radio advertising revenue in modern history in 1991.

While panic was sweeping through the radio universe, I was relatively calm. Having just gone through this in Houston, I wasn't seeing anything I hadn't seen before. I knew the station salespeople had to be sensitive to our clients struggling to keep their doors open, and management had to realize our salespeople were meeting increased objections and resistance and were subject to being discouraged. The sales staffs were working harder than ever just to stay even with the prior year's numbers, and the stations supported the effort with creativity and some fun. Just as we did back in Houston, Keymarket did more client entertaining, inviting clients to concerts with parties before and after, nights at the ballpark, dinners at the best restaurants. The activity all contributed to holding onto the clients and to maintaining spirit at the stations. This was also the time when we created another method to engage the salespeople further, a twist to the commission compensation system.

I landed in Memphis early in the evening. Our GM, Curt Peterson, and the stations' general sales manager, Ken Miller, picked me up at the airport, then the three of us headed to dinner. As we sat down, Ken was noticeably upset. "And to what do we owe your pleasant disposition?" I sarcastically asked. Ken shot back, "The salespeople just don't care. I work and work and work and give them ideas for their clients and go on calls with them and they just don't care." I said, "Ken, you're going to have to be more specific. What are you saying? What don't they care about?"

"Just this morning I announced in the sales meeting how we were doing against the sales budget for the month and what we had to do to make it. I wanted to see some fire, some enthusiasm, some indication that the staff was going to really get into high gear and go for it. I wanted to feel some energy. But all I got were blank stares. They just don't care."

I sat for a second and let Ken simmer down a bit and then asked him, "Why should they?"

I thought he was going to throw the breadbasket at me. "Why should they care? It's their livelihood. That's why?" Ken yelled.

"But why exactly should they care?" I started in again. "You stand up and announce the goal and what you want, but they hear it as your problem. What's in it for them?"

At that point, Curt took out his pen and spiral notebook and began to scribble. Ken and I looked over and saw him doodling numbers. Then Curt said, "What if we adjusted the commission plan?" As was standard in the radio business, we were paying our salespeople a percentage of their sales. The salespeople were paid as a share of what they brought in. Over the next hour, we cooked up the beginnings of a system that would pay different commission rates based on performance. The salesperson would start with a certain percentage, then when they achieved their individual goal for the month, the percentage went up (from dollar one), and when the station made its budget, the percentage would go up again.

We fine-tuned the plan over the next few days and had it ready to present to the staff during the goal-setting meetings for the following month. The sales staff was excited, and Ken now had a tool to help them see "why they should care" about the stations' budget.

After seeing this plan work in Memphis, we rolled the idea out to all the Keymarket stations. It was a way to involve the salespeople in what was up to now "management's problem."

λ

Back at the home office, the national recession led to more meetings with the finance committee about cutting expenses. My attitude was bad in these meetings, and I was sometimes accused of not being in touch with the harsh reality of the situation. But I was misunderstood. It was, and still is, my feeling that any idiot can cut expenses. It's especially easy if you have an HR department or outside consultant (George Clooney style) who can do the dirty work. I also know that most corporate staffs think the operators are just spending money with no thought and won't stop unless their hands are not just tied, but cut off. So this conflict always exists.

My operating belief then and now is to work hard with the station management team to set the tone, to form the culture of financial responsibility, and to lead by example. Then a company can accomplish the goal of running efficiently while at the same time being vibrant and competitive.

It is also essential to deal with each person as an individual. Some managers spend everything in sight without even realizing what they are doing. Some managers spend but always get a good return. Others are afraid to spend anything and then miss opportunities or, worse yet, hurt their market position.

Part of leadership is knowing how to give people equal treatment but understanding that this doesn't mean the same treatment. I attempted to give equal treatment by giving each person special treatment. When Gerald Getz in Wilkes Barre asked for money to buy a new station vehicle, I gave it to him. Other managers would complain to me that Gerald was favored, and it wasn't fair. Why couldn't the other managers have new promotional vehicles for their stations, too? I explained, "Every time I send Gerald fifty cents he sends me a dollar back. When you learn to do that, you'll get what you want."

I am 100 percent for expense management and cost controls and saving money wherever and whenever it is possible. I am 100 percent against cost cutting that makes the business look good for a few minutes without achieving any long-term benefit. Cuts that actually make it more difficult to operate. Cuts that hurt the ability to grow revenue and then solve the bottom line problem. Unless a business is growing revenue, the business will not improve profits. It doesn't matter what business it is. Saving your way to prosperity will not work.

$$\lambda$$

At Keymarket, the general managers and I worked together to develop a good plan up front and then worked the plan. We didn't want to be faced with making staff cuts that looked good on paper but hurt the overall effort. I learned to operate this way from making calls on the advertisers. The clients know when there are layoffs at TV, radio stations, and the newspapers, and they're keeping score. The clients legitimately ask, "How can you come in and preach about investing, preach about growing, preach about spending money to make money when at your station you are cutting people and services?"

When a meeting was called at the Keymarket corporate offices to reduce expenses in New Orleans on WWL, I showed up with a double bad attitude. The questions were predictable. Does WWL need this many news reporters? Does this time period need a live host, or can the station plug in some network show? Does WWL have to have three people hosting the pregame show on Sundays, or can it go with two hosts, or better yet, just one?

To be fair and balanced here, I admit I was not sensitive to the magnitude of the moment. Keymarket had been on a buying spree for a year, and now the economy was turning downward. Any reduction in Keymarket's operating income was going to make it tough to meet the company's debt obligations. But sometimes it's better to be ignorant or choose to be blind. I chose to remain blind. I excused myself from dealing with the facts: the realities of Keymarket's debt and loan agreements. Instead, I fought for what I felt in my heart was the right path to follow. I believed that if we succumbed to reducing costs, personnel, and services, the company would be in worse shape in a very short period. Within a few months, we'd be holding yet another meeting, calling for even more reductions.

On all counts, I was against any changes at WWL. I argued that the plan for the station was working. Keymarket had taken a station with low, nearly nonexistent morale and confidence, a station mired in mediocrity and self-pity, and was turning the situation around. In my final and perhaps most compelling assertion, I claimed that if Keymarket had any chance of servicing debt, holding off the banks in the tough economy, and saving the company, that chance was riding on the back of one radio station. WWL held all the potential. This one station had the inherent strength to grow revenue and exceed expectations in the face of recession and war. To make budget cuts now would only telegraph to the people of WWL and to the New Orleans market that Keymarket had lost faith, and thus, failure would become a self-fulfilling prophecy.

I may have been channeling Jimmy Stewart that day, but my impassioned plea hit the mark and we proceeded with no changes at WWL. This meant the pressure was on our manager, Johnny Andrews, and me to perform and meet the revenue growth objectives. I knew we would. And when the word got to Johnny that WWL had been spared any cost cutting and that the plan would remain intact, he didn't shudder from the responsibility. Johnny and his staff rose to the challenge with enthusiasm and led not only WWL but also the entire Keymarket group to new and higher levels of revenue and profitability.

As with most media news outlets, recession and war resulted in added tune-in to WWL. The station boasted an updated, more entertaining and contemporary approach to the news/talk format, and this was advertised on TV and outdoor. However, recruiting new and younger listeners was still a challenge. When the Gulf War began in January of 1991, WWL's sampling spiked immediately. Once we got them to sample, these new listeners became loyalists of the up-to-date 870AM. January of 1991 was the turning point, and the station never looked back.

As the ratings grew and our reputation flourished, WWL was now positioned as an institution more than a radio station. Naturally, a client summed it up best. Johnny Andrews and I sat down to lunch with Peter Mayer, the founder and head of Peter Mayer Advertising, a well-respected force in the marketplace.

"I want to personally congratulate you two for what you have done," Peter began. "For many years WWL radio has been in decline. Because of its history, because of its heritage, because of its meaning to our citizens, its decline was a black cloud over New Orleans. You have restored the pride. New Orleans feels good when WWL is recognized as first class. Thank you for what you have done."

Flying out of New Orleans that evening, I felt good that what we were doing was connecting and being noticed. However, at that very moment, I was on my way up to Pennsylvania where in Harrisburg our advertisers were singing a different tune.

CHAPTER 37

BOND, BRUCE BOND

WINK-104, the number one radio station in Harrisburg, Pennsylvania, was a monster. With great fanfare, Keymarket bought the station, then WTPA, in late 1984 and in early 1985, changed the format from album rock to all things to all people/full service/personality/AC/Top40, which generated an immediate and overwhelmingly positive reaction from listeners and advertisers. The station posted consistent double-digit audience shares, often approaching and occasionally hitting twenty, with dominance in all demographics male and female across all ages. WINK-104 was the market's most listened to station with the 12-34, 18-49, and 25-54 age groups, capturing a disproportionate share of the market's radio revenue—in other words, an enormous cash cow. I had nothing to do with building this station. It was running at full steam long before I was named company president. My responsibility was keeping it up, as the company's overall performance depended upon a robust WINK-104.

WINK-104 was starting to witness some previously unseen signs of revenue trouble. The national recession was part of the problem. Bernie Siegel had already alerted me of a business downturn and two of WINK's largest automotive accounts, Greg Sutliff and Klare Sunderland, were verifying it. The other source of the trouble was new and improved competition.

The beautiful music station, WHP-FM, had awakened and changed to an adult contemporary format. A station owned by the Presbyterian Church was sold to a commercial operator and started playing oldies. A 50,000-watt Class B FM just north of York, about fifteen miles south of us, was doing a version of CHR, impersonating the nationally acclaimed Power Pig from Tampa, Florida, and going directly after WINK's 12-24 year-old listeners. WINK-104 was being hit from all sides, but the biggest source of trouble was inside the station.

Bruce Bond was WINK-104's afternoon personality and program director from day one. As the station grew and the workload increased, Keymarket had put an operations manager in place, but Bruce still had a high degree of influence over the station and management, and felt free to do on the air whatever he saw fit. For the most part, this worked. Bruce was engaging, fun, outrageous, attention-getting, risqué, and cared about the community, all at the same time. He stole a number of bits from Howard Stern, whose show was only heard in New York back then. When people in Harrisburg listened to Bruce interviewing porn stars such as Marylyn Chambers and doing skits such as lesbian dial-a-date, listeners thought it was original. Bruce did a good job of executing these knock-offs, so for the most part Bruce's act was delivering listeners, advertisers, ratings, and revenue. In a focus group, the participants were trying to explain Bruce and as they went on and on, the moderator attempted to wrap up saying, "So Bruce Bond is . . ." A man at the end of the table said, "An ass." "So why does everyone listen?" To which a nice young lady at the center of the table replied, "Because he's *our* ass."

Bruce was a hometown hero, the kid everyone liked because, even though he'd do bad things, he had a good heart. And he did. There wasn't a major charity event to which Bruce Bond wouldn't give his personal time. He was wild, but he was also devoted to the market.

With the increase in competition, WINK-104 had to hunker down and ensure the sound was just right. This put a lot of pressure on the air staff, and everyone was handling it OK, except Bruce. Instead of doing just a little less and being more effective, he was doing more and more, saying more and more outrageous things, and it was starting to be a real turnoff. The thin line between those who listened every day because they loved him and those who listened every day because they hated him was now blurred. And the advertisers took notice. The WINK-104 salespeople always had to defend Bruce to clients about something or other. The clients would show concern about Bruce's antics and remarks, but knowing how strong Bruce was with the listeners, they would shrug and look the other way. Now with three new stations to choose from, the clients were experimenting with ways to avoid WINK's afternoon drive show.

Station management and WINK's programming consultant had been working with Bruce for months, trying to help him stay on track. With each passing day, Bruce listened to the coaching less and less.

Bruce's resistance to this direction caused the situation at WINK to deteriorate to such an extent that a decision had to be made. As much as I hated to do it, and as much as I knew that in the short term this would make a bad situation worse, I had to fire Bruce Bond.

Right away the sales staff, which had been threatening mutiny if something wasn't done about the Bruce problem, revolted. The sales people were looking for some kind of miracle. They didn't want Bruce to be fired. Now any problem they were having selling the station they blamed on me. I was supposed to fix this, not make things worse. The clients saw WINK as vulnerable. For years, they had accepted the station's rate increases because of WINK's dominance. Now the advertisers felt they were in the driver's seat. "You are not what you once were," a good client said to me. He was absolutely right. It just felt awful to hear it.

After Bruce's departure, WINK's programming staff worked doubly hard to make the station sound as good as it could. WINK-104's morning man, Tim Burns, performed better than ever and, looking back, deserves a ton of credit for keeping the station's audience numbers up. WINK's operations manager, John O'Dea, along with Frank Bell from Keymarket, fine-tuned the music for maximum appeal. During all this, WINK-104 remained number one in the market. The difference being WINK was no longer as dominant over the radio competitors, and this compression caused WINK's commercial rates to soften, leading to a decline in revenue and profits.

Bruce sat on the sidelines for a few months then went to work at an upstart AC station in New Orleans, coincidentally. But neither that station nor Bruce made any inroads.

In the fall of 1991, I gave Bruce a call just to say hello and suggested we get together sometime during one of my visits to New Orleans. He was open to it.

Several times that fall and early winter of 1992, we met face-to-face and talked about everything.

Now that time had passed, I found it easy to talk with Bruce about what had happened in Harrisburg, and how the future could be different. I let him know how much I respected his talent and how it would be terrific if somehow we could get back together. Finally, we got to the point of discussing Bruce's return to WINK-104. Bruce reacted positively and was excited. I believed he was sincere about wanting to return and make the station even better than it ever was.

This led to a meeting with station management and Frank Bell. At first, no one was too keen on the idea of rehiring Bruce, and I understood why. Management, along with the salespeople and the on-air staff, had been through the downside of Bruce's departure. They had dealt with all the negatives from the listeners, and the clients, and the falloff in the ratings. Now, months later, the station sounded great and everything was moving forward. The ratings weren't up to the highs of the past but were very good, and all the initial thunder of the new competition had subsided. I was proposing to turn everything upside down again.

All I asked was that management come up with the guidelines they would want to put in place should we bring Bruce back. The team responded in a very professional manner and produced a design for formatting the afternoon show that would work for everyone. I took the plan to New Orleans, sat down with Bruce, and once I got his buy-in we began to arrange for his comeback. The date was set, April 1, 1992.

Back at the station, all sorts of ideas were bandied about to reintroduce Bruce Bond. Teaser campaigns, billboards, riding into town in a limo, riding into town on a horse, all great thoughts. No one tactic struck me as perfect. Then it hit me. The best way to hype Bruce Bond's return to WINK-104 was no hype at all. We would do or say absolutely nothing. At 3:00 p.m. on April 1, 1992, Bruce Bond simply showed up and went on the air. I asked him not to even give his name at all that first day. Twenty minutes into the show, callers were on the air saying, "Is this, are you, is it Bruce Bond?" His distinctive voice and style made it impossible for them not to notice. WINK-104 got the best kind of hype there is: hype from the listeners.

I tried to do the same thing with the sales staff. I told the salespeople not to run out and be overly enthusiastic. This is the opposite of what I normally would want, but I didn't want to put the salespeople in a position of pushing Bruce, and the clients saying, "Yeah, we'll see how he does" and thus dampening their spirits.

Instead, the staff played it cool, and, in no time, the clients demanded to be on the air with increased schedules and higher rates and, of course, a strong presence in afternoon drive. The clients knew the return of Bruce was a big event and wanted to be a part of it.

Just as Bruce had intended, the show was better than ever, and he stayed at WINK-104 for another ten years. Keymarket sold WINK-104 in 1993, but I enjoyed knowing Bruce Bond was back on the station and continuing to dominate the market. Bruce and I had dinner one night years later and reminisced. I told Bruce he was the main character in my best and worst two days in radio. The worst being the day I had to fire him. The best being the day he returned.

CHAPTER 38

PRE-NEW ERA

B ack in Texas, in the summer of 1991, something happened that would eventually change everything. The recession and the Gulf War had left many operators devastated. This is when Steve Hicks and Hicks Broadcasting invented the LMA. This local marketing agreement allowed a station to sell all of its on-air time, commercial and programming, but not the station's FCC license, to another radio station. Some people referred to these as "lease deals." When news broke out of Austin that Steve had taken an underperforming FM under the wing of his successful FM operation, with no FCC transfer necessary, it sent shockwaves across the nation.

The immediate reaction was denial. "This can't be possible, it can't be legal," cried the broadcasters. But at Keymarket, we weren't calling our lawyers. We were calling every operator in every one of our markets looking for new combinations.

The underlying concept of the LMA was that an existing FM, adding a second FM, would benefit from the second FM's revenue stream, and by operating this second station for about half the cost of the first, immediately create additional cash flow.

Keymarket found an FM in New Orleans, KMEZ, owned by a local group of investors who had no previous radio experience. The station was running at a loss, and the investors were putting more of their own money in just to keep the lights on. The owners desperately wanted out, and Keymarket was there to help. Keymarket entered into an LMA with KMEZ and moved the station in with WWL and WLMG. All we did was relieve the owners of their expense obligations. Therefore, with Keymarket now running the operation of KMEZ, the owner's immediate benefit was the elimination of all costs. Then in exchange for paying the owner's a monthly fee, Keymarket got the option to buy KMEZ at a predetermined price. Buying radio stations was like going down to Aaron's Rent to Own.

Keymarket selected the Satellite Music Network's urban adult contemporary format for KMEZ with the idea there were plenty of shares available, as market leaders WYLD and WQUE were aiming at the younger urban audience. Thus, Keymarket added a new signal with no investment but a monthly payment to the owners plus the amount of the power bill. Back at the corporate office, I was called into another meeting. This time the question was how to create the revenue stream for the new station, KMEZ.

By this time, I learned enough about combo selling not to fool around. My own experience as a salesperson, and the recent events in Austin with the addition of the AM, gave me all the education I needed on this subject.

I was prepared for the meeting and stated my case clearly. "There are only two options, and only two," I said. "One, hire a separate sales staff to deal exclusively with the new station, or two, cement the two FM stations together: WLMG/KMEZ as one. No separate rates. One rate, two stations. No deviation."

I described WLMG/KMEZ as a suit, not a coat and pants available as separates. You want the coat? You buy the suit. Instead of asking, "You want fries with that?" (which I knew the salespeople did not like doing), this is a Happy Meal, fries included.

This approach turns the transaction around and makes it easier. If someone says they do not want the fries, then take them off the plate, but the price of the platter remains the same. So the customer says, "OK, then, give me the fries."

In New Orleans, during September of 1991, there was really only one way to go: combining and cementing the two stations together. There was no available cash for fronting a new sales team. So the next question was regarding price. What do we do to the existing rates on WLMG? My answer was "Nothing. Let everyone know that when they buy WLMG, the new KMEZ comes with it. No added cost. 'Lagniappe,' as they say in Louisiana. Let's just get everyone on. KMEZ is a brand new station. Let's avoid any confusion and resistance from the salespeople, eliminate the stress of the evaluation process, and make it easy for the clients to buy into it."

I actually stole this plan from Viacom. When Keymarket bought Viacom's Memphis stations, the manager told me how, when their company bought an AM to go with their existing FM, they got the advertisers to buy the AM. The salespeople started by duplicating on the AM, for no additional cost, the schedules the clients were buying on the FM. That way, there were no objections to the AM being added. The clients were happy to have the second station and to be airing twice the number of commercials. Then as time went on, sales management just raised the rates gradually and steadily but kept the two stations together and kept the advertisers using both.

When I introduced the concept of WLMG and KMEZ being sold together as one, I got some quizzical looks at the Keymarket corporate office, but at the stations in New Orleans, Johnny Andrews loved the idea and so did the sales staff. WLMG's revenue went up right away because, with the added value of a second station, WLMG was now winning the close calls, the coin flips against WLTS, the AC competitor, and getting on more buys. As KMEZ rose in the ratings, and as inventory tightened on WLMG, the rates went up, and fast, but we already had the clients with us. The clients liked the idea of an ethnically balanced FM/FM buy because they were getting good results. The sales staff did a fabulous job with the clients and the plan worked beautifully.

⅄

As 1991 ended, it looked as if the economic skies were about to brighten. Keymarket had momentum. Johnny Andrews was seeing rapid growth in New Orleans, even before adding KMEZ, so the LMA was a sweetener. WKRZ in Wilkes Barre was ahead of plan, San Bernardino was exploding, the format change in Charlotte took hold, and Bruce Bond was on his way back to Harrisburg. Memphis, with new manager Curt Peterson, was moving forward, and Texas born and raised Lon Bason was coming into his own and proving to be a solid replacement for Johnny Andrews in Austin. To capitalize on the strength we had built and prepare for the year ahead, we asked the 100 Questions.

⋏

On a sunny Saturday in August of 1991, I sat outside on our back porch at home with a pile of files. As the day went on, I combed through the material looking for commonalities in behavior across Keymarket's eight markets. I checked for all the things the stations were doing to move the needle: recruiting, training, organization, systems, promotions, marketing pieces, client relations. Then I put all of it in order in the form of questions. This became "The 100 Questions—a 100-point checklist to be sure your stations are ready for 1992."

I hit the road and went through The 100 Questions with our managers and sales managers. What the 100 Questions provided was a list of best practices and a self-accountability tool. Each market had the same checklist, although each market's emphasis was different. In meeting with the managers, we would go through the Questions and identify what items should be done to improve each station. Some items on the list of 100 would get attention, and some would be put aside for another day. Action plans were tailored to each market's objectives based on position and personnel.

The 100 Questions put the spotlight on process as opposed to results (how much business came in today?). As management concentrated on process and became more fundamentally sound, the results kept improving. As America came out of its economic doldrums, radio revenue across the US rebounded and finished 1992 up 2 percent over 1991. Thanks to the 100 Questions, Keymarket's revenue, in 1992, was up 26 percent.

CHAPTER 39

PRE-NEW ERA, PHASE TWO

If anything is certain in this world, it's that the FCC will always jump on the caboose of a runaway train. By the beginning of 1993, LMAs were being done everywhere. Washington came up with new rules so that the commission could get some control back. The first FCC move was to allow duopoly. This allowance permitted companies to own two AMs and two FMs in the same market as long as the group of stations did not exceed a combined audience share of twenty. Later on, the cap was extended to four AM and four FM with certain revenue restrictions. This all climaxed with the Telecom bill in 1996, leaving the state of affairs we see in the industry today.

ᐦ

As 1992 concluded, the word came down from Keymarket's private equity sponsor, TA and Associates, that the company was to get its markets in order. In other words, find an operator to combine with in each market or sell: get out of that market. Keymarket added stations in three markets and exited five markets. Then, as 1993 got underway, the company looked to expand again. Now we would only enter a market where we could buy at least two FMs and, preferably two AMs, as well.

The first attempt to add a market within this new paradigm was in Toledo, Ohio. Keymarket simultaneously entered into purchase agreements with two separate sellers. We were set to buy WVKS-FM from Nobel Broadcast and two stations from Commonwealth Broadcasting: WSPD-AM and WLQR-FM. The deals would give us two FMs and WSPD-AM, a strong performer in the news/ talk format. Kerby, Frank Bell, and I scoured the Toledo Arbitron rating books, current and past, and determined that the stations Keymarket was set to purchase never exceeded a combined eighteen share of audience (comfortably below the FCC cap of twenty). The agreements were signed and filed at the FCC. Sixty days later, as the company was anticipating approval of the transfers, we received an urgent call from our FCC attorney telling us the process was put on hold. There was a petition to deny filed at the commission by Midwestern Broadcasting, owner of a competing Toledo FM, on the grounds that the three stations had combined shares exceeding the 20 percent cap. Midwestern Broadcasting also owned Stratford Research, and Stratford produced a study showing twenty plus shares for our proposed group. Keymarket and the company attorneys argued that Stratford Research had no standing in the industry as a barometer of ratings, but the FCC was paralyzed. Not knowing what to do, the commission did nothing. The purchase agreements eventually passed the expiration dates, and the deals went away. Keymarket could have spent a lot of time and money fighting this one but decided to throw in the towel and move on.

The company ended up with a better deal for two AMs and two FMs in Buffalo and a deal in Nashville for two FMs and an AM. Shortly thereafter, we began putting together a combination of two AMs and two FMs in Greenville-Spartanburg, South Carolina and shed no tears over Toledo.

An off-strategy, but highly profitable, opportunity came our way from Fred Sands, the real estate mogul in Los Angeles. Fred owned an AM and FM, and as radio was not his primary concern, he was thinking of cashing out and taking advantage of the stations' appreciation in value.

KNAC-FM was licensed to Long Beach. It put a minor signal into LA and showed modest ratings in the LA Arbitron. The format was heavy metal, and it catered to that niche, which was vibrant in Southern California. KNAC was well known among rock music fans worldwide, as the station was credited with breaking Gun 'n' Roses.

Working with our team at KNAC (Gary Price, Brian Schock, and John Squyers) added to my appreciation for the value of knowing your audience and matching it up with the right advertisers. By the nature of the station, many clients in Los Angeles had no interest in KNAC. The sales department smartly worked businesses who knew attracting KNAC listeners would add to their bottom line. The salespeople ignored much of the general market retail, the department stores, and grocery markets and concentrated on categories such as convenience stores, beverages, fast food, entertainment, musical instrument stores, and automotive, particularly imports. To advertisers in these categories, what mattered wasn't how many listeners KNAC had but who these listeners were. KNAC listeners expressed their loyalty by responding to the commercials.

KBLA-AM was programmed under an LMA by Radio Korea. Because of FCC foreign ownership restrictions, Jay Lee the CEO of Radio Korea could not own KBLA. Keymarket was the licensee and responsible to the FCC. Radio Korea provided the programming from its studios in Koreatown, just off Western Avenue in Los Angeles. Keymarket retained two minutes of commercial inventory each hour and General Manager Ron Thompson sold these to national accounts who desired reaching the Korean population. Jay Lee and his staff sold commercials to the local merchants in Koreatown. My role included meeting with Jay a few times a year. He was very gracious, taking me to his favorite Korean restaurants, where, of course, he had to do all the ordering. I accepted whatever was served, never having any idea what I was enjoying.

CHAPTER 40

RIVER CITY

After two years of deal making, the Keymarket reorganization resulted in a seven-market, twenty-six-station group. At the same time, the economy had rebounded, partly growing out of the depths of 1991 and partly from the early stages of the new technology revolution. Radio revenue was up nicely as well, so it was the perfect scenario for Keymarket's private equity sponsor, TA and Associates, to make their exit and cash out. Keymarket's options were to sell the stations (as a group or as individual markets), or find new investors. One such possibility was the public market. The IPO market was hot and, because of deregulation and consolidation, radio stocks and IPOs were riding high with the bull market. We decided to take Keymarket public. The prospectus was prepared and all the participants, the bankers, investment bankers, advisors, and lawyers lined up with their hands out. We were just about to board the plane and take off for our road show when the stock market underwent a correction. A quick calculation showed that while we would still sell the same number of shares, the price would be slightly reduced, and that reduction was enough to leave us coming up short in paying off TA. This is like selling your house and writing a check to your lender at closing to pay off your mortgage. No fun for us. So six months of work went good-bye, and it was back to the drawing board to line up equity investors.

We met with a number of private equity firms and other broadcasters to discuss various partnerships. One such meeting led to serious consideration.

Barry Baker and Larry Marcus had formed River City Broadcasting in 1989 to purchase KDNL-TV30 in St. Louis. KDNL was an independent station full of reruns, cartoons, and old movies. The station was owned by Viacom and was out of step with their corporate image. It was a perfect point of entry to television ownership for River City Broadcasting and proved to be excellent timing.

River City immediately affiliated with the new FOX network. At this time, the network offered two hours a night of fresh first-run programming just a few nights a week. This was five years before FOX did its NFL deal. To a station like KDNL, FOX, with its exciting line-up of *The Simpsons*, *Beverly Hills 90210*, and *The Tracy Ullman Show*, was magic.

And one more sprinkle of serendipity. Nielsen was about to convert its TV ratings methodology in St. Louis from diary to meter. This would mean more response from younger viewers. The meter would favor the FOX network, and stations like KDNL could expect higher ratings.

Barry Baker, who had operated radio stations for years before entering the television business, took all the pages from his local radio sales playbook and adapted them for KDNL. An aggressive local sales effort was unusual in television at that time. The revenue growth on KDNL was swift and significant.

KDNL's immediate success led to River City's expansion into six additional television markets. Kerby and I had known Barry Baker from his radio days and had always maintained a professional friendship. Keymarket decided to sell the company to River City and their private equity sponsor, Boston Ventures. Under this new ownership structure, Keymarket would continue to operate the radio stations.

The River City-Keymarket combination seemed like a good fit to me. The radioesque sales philosophies of River City would mesh with what Keymarket was already doing, and I was personally excited about the opportunity to learn more about the TV business from the inside.

The organizational plan was to keep the radio offices in Georgia, but, as the time of closing the deal drew near, I volunteered to move to St. Louis. I thought it would be better for the company and for me to be housed at the main head-quarters rather than an outpost.

Kerby understood and endorsed the idea, but Barry Baker was cool. He put me off and said not to do anything right away; I would have an office in St. Louis and could come in as often as I liked, but that I should not do anything permanent. One thing I didn't know was that Baker wasn't planning to be in St. Louis much longer.

At Keymarket, the radio division of River City Broadcasting, it was pretty much business as usual. We submitted budgets to River City for approval, and we were accountable to Boston Ventures, but our day-to-day operations didn't change. I still visited the radio stations, worked with the managers, and called on our clients.

In July of 1995, upon closing on the deal to buy Keymarket, River City Broadcasting entered into discussions to sell River City, television and radio, to Sinclair Broadcast Group in Baltimore. So just eleven months after Keymarket became part of River City, we all became part of Sinclair on June 1, 1996. There was no moving to Missouri. The Keymarket gang was on the way to Maryland.

PART FIVE
THE NEW ERA

CHAPTER 41

Sinclair Broadcast Group

Sinclair Broadcast Group started as a family business by Julian Sinclair Smith. As the torch was passed to the next generation and David Smith assumed leadership, the company expanded and very aggressively pursued a consolidation strategy. The company had gone public in 1995 and buying River City was a perfect piece in Sinclair's growth story. That story continues to this day, and Sinclair is the largest group operator of television stations in the United States.

Life evolved as the Keymarket stations were now part of a public company. The name Keymarket was dropped, and we were simply the radio division of Sinclair Broadcast Group. At this point, Robin Smith was brought in as chief financial officer for radio, as we needed additional strength and leadership to meet the exacting reporting standards of the public arena.

I was experiencing the challenges of managing a public company. It forced me to look ahead at all times and think carefully about any decision being made. I learned to envision how any moves were likely to play out in the long term, but simultaneously keep the stations and the general managers focused on the monthly and quarterly revenue and profit objectives.

⅄

The radio audience was not aware of any of these internal changes. Listeners rarely, if ever, comment or care about who owns the radio stations they use. The listeners either like what they are hearing or don't. Same with clients. The adver-tisers know their salesperson, maybe a manager, maybe someone in production and copy, maybe a station personality and, of course, the client knows whether their invoices are correct or not. In most cases, when stations change hands, it makes no difference to the advertisers. As Keymarket made the transitions to River City and then Sinclair, our dealings with the radio stations' clients didn't change at all. The process remained the same: make the calls, do a good presen-tation, ask for the order.

There were, however, changes being brought about by the massive radio station consolidation set loose with the Telecom bill passed by Congress in early 1996. Over a period of only a few months, there was tectonic movement affect-ing every city in America. Companies were now operating what became known as "clusters," groups of four to eight stations in each market. This change caused advertisers to notice and respond.

⅄

On a visit to our radio stations in Buffalo, my first stop was the stations' sales office. Sitting at the table were the general manager, the director of sales, and the local sales manager. The three of them were having a low volume, but passion-ate, debate. One of the market's biggest advertisers, a furniture store, was about to make an annual radio buy and our stations' sales practices were in question.

Although our Buffalo operation was now a six-station group, we still had four separate sales staffs; only two small AMs were sold in combination with larger stations. This particular client was being called on by four different peo-ple. I believed this method was correct because the radio stations were serving four very distinct consumer groups, and in order for the stations to be presented properly and to be adequately valued by the client, there had to be four custom presentations.

The radio market in Buffalo was primarily owned by three companies: Sinclair, CBS, and Citadel. The client being discussed had just announced it was going to buy two of the three groups, and our managers were talking about who from our group would make the pitch since the client didn't want to see sales-people for each individual station.

While the radio industry was in the process of consolidating and assembling combos and clusters, media buyers had made it quite clear and told us at every opportunity, "When we are placing buys, we are only going to buy stations on a station's merits. No way are we going to be forced into buying any combinations or groups."

Now there was an about-face. Very quickly, clients had figured out how to turn the whole situation around and use it against us. Pit the groups against each other. Instantly, I had a flashback. Radio's new selling condition took me back to an afternoon in the early 1980s.

I was with a friend who worked for a sizable advertising agency as an account executive. He was showing me around the shop. We stopped outside the door of the broadcast TV network buyer, Nancy, who was busy at work talking with the reps from ABC, CBS, and NBC.

Nancy told each of her sales reps that the buy was going to be finalized that afternoon, so they had to be on their toes and ready to act quickly. The buyer announced she was going to buy two of the three networks. Within minutes, Nancy had quotes and began to make her callbacks. First, she called NBC. Nancy informed the rep that presently she was going with ABC and CBS. She got a rebid from NBC, then called CBS. Nancy told the rep she was buying ABC and NBC. CBS rebid, and the buyer called ABC to tell the rep she was buying CBS and NBC. ABC rebid and this round-robin tournament went on for the better part of the afternoon, Nancy driving rates down with every phone call. Flash forward now almost fifteen years to the situation in Buffalo.

My memory of Nancy made me fear for what was going to happen to radio. Instead of presenting the value of individual stations, a value based on the desirability and quality of the station's audience, stations were going to be clumped together. I could see that once radio stations stopped selling the advertisers on individual consumer groups and the unique ability of certain stations to deliver for the advertiser, radio would diminish to a commodity and fall prey to being eaten alive by talented, astute, experienced buyers. I couldn't be surprised. Clients are masters at purchasing goods and services. Radio was now another opportunity to put their skills to use.

Fortunately, we were able to hold our ground in Buffalo. The stations' director of sales made the case to the head of the advertising department at the client level for separate presentations. The client knew the value of the stations, and so we were successful that particular day, but I could feel the landscape changing.

ᛉ

The overall economy in the late 90s was very strong. This drove advertising expenditures to new highs, and radio revenue was growing at a disproportionate pace. No one felt compelled to address the issue of how clients had learned to deal with radio stations selling as groups in a given market. At the same time, radio's commercial inventory expanded. It was the dirty little secret that turned out to be not so little.

ᛉ

As the huge public radio companies held their conference calls announcing quarterly results during 1997 and 1998, the Wall Street analysts were giddy over the double-digit revenue increases. Corks were popping from New York to Texas. The radio station consolidation strategy was declared a success. And no one, not one time, did anyone on an analyst conference call ask, "How many commercials are you running?"

Radio clusters were competing with one another, and in each market, the game was being played to win share. Demand was strong so the volume held. In certain major cities, the dot-com category was adding 15-20 percent in new dollars. Radio stations began to lose self-control and the commercial unit loads went up.

Deregulation allowed the purchase of competing stations, so stations stopped worrying about commercials and loosened the reins. Eight minutes went to twelve minutes went to fifteen minutes. . . . The analysts covering radio for the banks and Wall Street knew this, but it was never talked about. Short-term thinking at its worst.

A freshman economics student can explain that during a time of high demand the supply must be managed. If not, when the demand softens—which the laws of economics dictate it eventually will—the floor will fall out.

Although a relatively small group, Sinclair Radio was doing very well. The radio division was producing a substantial up-tick in revenue and cash flow to the point that in several quarters radio was responsible for the entire amount of earnings growth at Sinclair.

The company had never been in radio before. Radio wasn't really in Sinclair's plans. The radio group just came along with the River City TV acquisition, but Sinclair sure liked radio's performance. So much so that the radio division expanded nicely while under Sinclair. Radio added five markets, buying Heritage Media in Milwaukee, St. Louis, and Kansas City and purchasing Norfolk and Greensboro from Max Media. By 1999, Sinclair radio was the proud owner of fifty stations in ten markets.

Part of the Sinclair purchase of River City called for Barry Baker to come in as CEO. I was radio COO, and later named CEO of radio, but I also attended and participated in the television management meetings. Being in these meetings allowed me to see how the TV stations operated and get to know the TV station GMs, sales managers, and executive team.

After almost three years at Sinclair, Barry Baker departed to join USA Networks. I was on the road when this was announced but called the chairman, David Smith, first thing the next morning and set a date to meet that Saturday. At this meeting, I pitched David on running TV while continuing to run radio. I was enthusiastic about operating the TV stations and looked forward to an opportunity to adapt radio's aggressive sales excitement to television. David and I met half a dozen times over the next 100 days, and finally he said, "Yes, let's do this." I was set to be named CEO of television at the company management and sales meeting coming up in two weeks. However, before there was any public announcement about my additional role, something else popped up.

入

By the spring of 1999, radio was experiencing the last wave of consolidation. Sinclair's radio division represented choice markets, top-notch facilities, and strong revenue and cash flow. All the big radio companies were sending Sinclair offers to buy the radio group. It was such a frenzy that some of the offers would sail in by fax, handwritten.

One Friday morning, I got a message from David Smith's assistant labeled urgent. I was visiting stations in Milwaukee that day but heading back to Baltimore in the afternoon. When I got to the office at about 6:00 p.m., David was waiting for me. "There's been a development," said David in his usual deadpan delivery. He went on, "We have a solid offer for the radio division, from a solid company, and it's too good to pass up." As it turned out that offer was passed up when, a few weeks later, someone else arrived with a higher bid. Sinclair ended up selling the radio stations primarily to Entercom with a spin here and there to Emmis and Susquehanna in transactions completed by the close of 1999.

I was able to bring several colleagues from the radio division with me: Robin Smith as VP/finance, Carla Phillips as controller, and Jeff Sleete as VP/sales. These radio transfers worked alongside the existing television team of VP/Engineering Del Parks, VP/Programming Bill Butler, HR Director Don Thompson, and General Counsel Barry Faber. I felt good that we had a quality team in place to tackle the new challenges.

CHAPTER 42

Television Time

My appointment as CEO/television was announced at the annual managers meeting in early June 1999. I had been to these meetings before as the "radio guy," but this was something new and exciting. Sinclair owned or operated sixty television stations in forty markets. The markets were divided into five regions, so I set meetings with the regional directors and their general managers. The purpose was to let the television managers know what I believed in and how I saw us moving forward. Being lifelong TV people, many were skeptical. How will this radio guy know what to do?

I stuck to the basics. I briefly explained my background and my belief that our success would be determined by how well we served our advertisers. Sinclair's VP/programming, Bill Butler, had total command of the TV programming syndication market, and I felt he needed to be given complete authority and my unqualified endorsement. I told the GMs not to worry about programming. "Bill's in charge," I said. I could tell giving up programming control irked many of the TV general managers. They wanted to set the schedules for their stations, but sixty stations, each doing its own thing, just wasn't working. Sinclair was handicapped with too much old programming on the shelf; shows that were purchased and not running anywhere anymore but still being paid for. These program liabilities were costing Sinclair a fortune. The company was in a position, due to its size and scope, to make efficient programming purchases across its platform. The greater good was to let Bill handle the programming. (Over the next couple of years, the company reduced the program payments line dramatically.) Besides, I wanted the GM's to concentrate on sales.

I put together a much scaled-down version of the 100 Questions. I chose 10 basics that I looked at as the foundation of a successful sales organization. Implementing these points would get the general plan in motion. The business was running about 50 percent local and 50 percent national. In short order, the managers and I set our sights on increasing local and shifting the balance to 75/25. Over the following months, as I visited the Sinclair stations and talked with the salespeople, we started moving in the right direction. When salespeople would tell me their stories, how tough it was on the street and the objections they got, I had a standard comeback. I told them, "I've been selling radio for twenty-two years and never once met a prospect who didn't want to be on television."

Sure there was more competition in the TV arena than ever before, but the idea of being on television still arouses the emotion and fires the imagination of business owners. It sounds as if I am oversimplifying, but really, everyone wants to be on television.

⋏

An old cliché says success comes when good work meets good fortune. The first tangible signs of success from this new attitude came in the first quarter of 2000, and it came because of the performance of KDNL in St. Louis. The general manager was Tom Tipton. I first knew Tom in the 1980s when he was a rookie salesman at our radio stations. Tom and his team at KDNL were always good workers; all they needed was a little good fortune. In October of 1999, as we were preparing the budget for 2000, it was noted that as an ABC affiliate, KDNL would be carrying the Super Bowl. I flippantly chimed in, "And the St. Louis Rams will be in the game, so let's plan for all the additional revenue." Everyone laughed. We budgeted for the Super Bowl, but not for the Rams. No one in the world expected the Rams to make the playoffs, much less the Super Bowl. They didn't even have a quarterback. Their starter was hurt and the team had to go to the Arena League to get somebody. Lo and behold, the Rams not only made it to the Super Bowl, but also won the Super Bowl. KDNL revenue skyrocketed, leading the company to overachieve its budget for the quarter and send the year off to a great start. A funny but factual story that shows sometimes good work does team up with good fortune.

▲

Several years earlier, when I was getting acquainted with the River City operation, I noted a relationship the group had with a sales consultant, Phillip J. LeNoble. Philip was like Kevin Sweeney in that he was dedicated to local selling. He differed in that he had a standardized course called System 21 for training salespeople and developing presentations for prospects. System 21 was essentially founded on the principle of analytically assessing the prospect's market position, their objectives, how the business allocates their advertising budget and then proposing a reallocation to better achieve their objectives. The proposal was then spiced with creative to get the client excited—that combination of logic and emotion, once again. I saw that even though the initial fact-finding meeting, which Philip labeled a Data Base call, took a great deal of time, once that was accomplished, the sale had a better than 50 percent chance of closing. Since direct salespeople celebrate a 25 percent closing ratio and most are in the 10-20 percent range, the success rate of System 21 made it very attractive. Sales people were unnerved at first about the work involved and some of the arithmetic took time to learn, but once a salesperson got a little experience and practice, they took to it. System 21 was used by a number of River City markets, and some were still using it as part of Sinclair. I encouraged more markets to use Philip's services as it fit in perfectly with our quest to grow local revenue.

System 21 helped us actually bring in new direct revenue, which television stations rarely did. In their defense, TV is in such high demand from national and large local clients through agencies that working direct is not a priority. Viewers see commercials for direct accounts in daytime and overnight but not much in prime time.

▲

With our team gelling, and the Sinclair sales effort gaining momentum, I was able to become more attentive to a new category of client: Wall Street. Being

187

in the spotlight of a public company meant more selling of a different kind. It meant more meetings, conferences, and occasionally, being grilled by the analysts and bankers. I had a taste of selling on Wall Street as head of radio, being on the quarterly calls, and presenting at the company's annual meeting, but now as CEO/television, I was at a new level. This is when I first got to know Pat Talamantes.

Pat was chief financial officer/television, so we would spend quite a bit of time together. He and I came from different places. I was a disc jockey who morphed into a salesman who woke up one day as the CEO of a television group. Pat was a graduate of Stanford with an MBA from Wharton who came up through the ranks in banking. We were either going to be an oil and water mix or collaborate like Lennon and McCartney. Good news for me it was the latter; we complemented each other perfectly. Pat is now the President and CEO of the McClatchy Company, the third largest newspaper company in America. I value greatly the time we spent working together. Pat taught me the ins and outs of how the financial community views companies and investments. Pat always knew what information was important to the Wall Street analysts. This enabled me to structure the company's presentations to focus on the key points of Sinclair's operations and showcase the company's initiatives. My confidence in delivering these presentations came from knowing that Pat had us completely and correctly prepared. I am grateful to have been a colleague of Pat's, and I'm proud to call him a friend.

$$\lambda$$

After five years at Sinclair Broadcast Group, I sensed it was time to go on to something new. I didn't know what that something new was going to be. I just felt the need for a new challenge. I submitted my resignation and worked for ninety days as per the notice period required by my employment agreement.

The knowledge I gained during my time in television cannot be overstated. Particularly now as the content versus distribution debate rages on. Through firsthand practical operating experience, I developed an understanding of the subtleties of the relationships between television stations, the networks, the cable companies, and the satellite distributors, as well as the studios and program suppliers. All must thrive for the business to move forward and for the viewers and advertisers to be served. New technology and aggressive entrepreneurs will always be disrupting the status quo. Just when it appears calm, there will intrude a new content creator or distribution method. Having been on the inside helps me sort through it all and keep the issues in perspective. Reading stories in *Forbes* or the *Wall Street Journal* can never take the place of being there.

The same can be said regarding the financial community. My time in the public arena and having responsibility for operating a multibillion-dollar enterprise gave me a new appreciation for the thought process, motivations, and pressures of the banks and investment firms. Talking with these people directly, and getting to know many of them personally, allowed me a firsthand education.

CHAPTER 43

TIME OUT

Special Report #5: Tables Turned

Moving to Baton Rouge as a general manager benefitted me by allowing me to see the sales process from the opposite side of the desk. I turned into a client, the prospect salespeople wanted to see. Equipment manufacturers, office supply companies, sales training services, programming advisors, real estate agents, TV stations, newspapers, outdoor companies were all ringing to get my attention. Being a client opened my eyes in a very different way to the challenges salespeople face but also showed me how the best salespeople succeed. My hope was to be able to pass some of these lessons along to the salespeople in our stations, and I routinely made it a topic of discussion in our sales meetings.

There was a headline I used when telling stories of being a client:

"Ninety-five percent of those who claim to be in the sales profession are not even in the game. Only five percent are worthy of the name salesperson."

⅄

The message I was trying to send is that with a little work, a little thought, and the dedication to be a professional, a salesperson can gain admission to the 5 percent. It's a small club, but like that old saying, "There's no traffic jam on the extra mile." I don't mean to say it's easy to enter the 5 percent but, with 95 percent of the competition wandering around aimlessly, the odds are good. Clients want to deal with Five Percenters but finding them in the sea of salespeople takes work and a lot of patience.

When I first became a client, it was pre-Internet. The most common form of non-face-to-face contact was the telephone. Second to that would have been regular mail. Once or twice a day a stack of mail would be placed on my desk. It was the mark of an effective executive to choose a certain time each day to go through the mail all at once. "Doing the mail" it was called. The most efficient executives never touched a piece of paper more than once. For example, a letter would be read and a decision made on the spot to do one of the following:

A. Throw it away (this was the overwhelming majority).
B. Attach a note and send to someone else to read and act on.
C. Attach a note of reply to the sender.
D. Place it in a file (this was for government forms, executed contracts, etc.).
E. Hold for further review.

If out of 100 pieces of mail there were more than two *e*'s, it meant the executive wasn't doing the mail properly, not being efficient.

Selling goods or services through the mail was difficult. Some preselling could be done, some following up, gaining familiarity, positioning for a future call, but initiating an order? No chance.

Five Percenters knew how to use the mail effectively. They would start by defining its purpose. Was the mail piece simply for making an impression? Was it to tease the prospect of potential benefit? Was it to confirm an appointment or set the time of a future event? All positive uses of the mail and all with next steps of their own. To a Five Percenter, the mail was a tool that, when used properly and with a purpose, would achieve a specific result.

⅄

There are those miraculous occasions when a salesperson can catch someone on the phone but most of the time it's "leave a message." Before the age of voicemail, messages were taken by someone in the office by hand and written on a slip of paper. As the client, when I'd return to my office late afternoon, I'd be met with a pile of these messages, far too many for time to allow me to return. I, like all clients, had to have some mechanism to manage this. I separated all the slips into As, Bs and Cs:

- As were people I knew and people I wanted to talk to, people I was already doing business with or people with whom I was in the process of developing a relationship.
- Bs were those I was mildly interested in but were neither important nor urgent.
- Cs were people I had never heard of or to whom I had no compelling reason to talk.

In returning calls, I'd start with the As and then move on to the Bs and would very rarely have time to get to the Cs. I'd leave them for the next day, but at the end of the week, I tossed out any leftover Cs. Sorry to admit this, but I was responsible to my superiors or shareholders, and in their interest, I had to manage my time. So, no time for Cs.

I tell this story so salespeople can get a feel for the client and how they deal with their own time. So often I hear salespeople whining about clients who won't take or return their calls. This is what it's like on the other end of those calls.

λ

Progress meant the introduction of overnight mail and then the fax. Overnight mail didn't matter too much; it sped up the delivery of certain items but didn't alter the decision process. The fax changed things because, instead of mail showing up once or twice a day, it was now delivered in a steady stream. I was forced to think more clearly. I had to remind myself constantly just because the transmission was immediate that it did not dictate an immediate response. My job was to manage myself. Certainly, if something were important *and* urgent, it would receive the required reply. Otherwise, I had to use the same process with these fax communications as in dealing with regular mail.

Next came voicemail. This cut way down on message slips and was the first step toward the massive downsizing of secretarial pools at most corporations.

"You have forty-two new messages." Calling into the voicemail system and hearing this upped my heart rate and put me in action mode. I had to get through forty-two messages, but be sure to get to the ones I needed and the messages I wanted. Voicemail killed the Cs. With the push of a button, the Cs were either deleted or, at best, routed to someone else's voice mailbox. Under the old system, a C may have survived and even been replied to on a slow day. Now, C messages were finished.

This created the need for a new skill among the Five Percenters: leaving good voicemail. The Five Percenters are always prepared with a clear, concise voicemail message meant to make an impression or trigger a return call. A fumbling, mumbling message is sure to be erased. A lame, "this is so and so, please call me" got the same treatment.

The plus of voicemail was when a Five Percenter knew how to use it that I could use it with them. We could set and confirm appointments, determine agenda items, transmit copy information, even to the point of placing and confirming orders. As with regular mail, the Five Percenter had a tool in voicemail that, when used with purpose, was an aid to the sales process and a time-saver.

Then came the communication breakthrough that continues to be the most vexing method: email.

I'll just stick to basic email here. Email has branched out to texting and tweeting—and who knows what else by now—but the initial presence of email was the big game changer. With email, there came a decline in regular mail and a decline in phone calls. On the surface, it would seem that email would have made buyers and sellers more efficient, but is that what happened?

There are two aspects of dealing with email: volume and timing. With email, the volume of attempted communication erupted. I would venture to guess, in my own experience as a client, the volume of email is at least tenfold the volume of phone calls and regular mail put together prior to 1995. It's so easy for someone to send off an email; no dialing and trying to get through, no paper, no envelope, no stamps or postage machine, the sheer volume mounts by the second.

And this mounts again as others open their mail and decide they must reply to all, or cc everyone on all of their email.

On the receiving end, what is seen when looking at the inbox? A screen of type that all looks the same. No different sizes of envelopes, no different colors, no different typefaces on the outside. At least with voicemail, the sound of the human voice helps distinguish one from another. A look at the email inbox says they are all the same. Returning to the office and seeing a screen or scrolling on a handheld device while on the move, who gets through? As a client, I had to hope I could see, find, and then open the As.

I am obsessed with finding the As. It is very hard to pick them out of the maze on my screen, and I am in constant fear of missing one. So with email, it's all about the As. When it comes to the Bs, if time permits, I may open these just to see what's there but then either forward to someone else or delete. Ah, the delete key. The Cs get deleted without ever being opened. The Cs are just what's left over. No time for Cs.

A client has to manage the inbox. Sometimes managing the inbox can be a full-time job. Email time never ends; it is nonstop. Unlike regular mail that came in volume but all at once, email shows up every few seconds. The bell chimes—instant distraction. I have seen clients spend literally the entire day reacting to these bells. I know I have committed the same crime. Luckily, I was able to self-help myself by relegating my email activity to certain times of the day. Being a constant air traveler helped for a while. Now with Wi-Fi on board, even that barrier has been removed. Once again, the client must get control and manage their time. It is essential to the client's mental and business survival.

The Five Percenter knows this and uses email wisely. You won't find Five Percenters firing off aimless emails just hoping to get a prospect to pay attention to them.

With the severe reduction of phone calls, I made a pledge to myself to return all calls. The volume of phone calls is manageable, so I know I can keep this promise, and I like talking to salespeople who have the guts to call. This doesn't mean these salespeople are all Five Percenters. No, I still talk with many in the larger group. They get me on the phone only to reveal themselves as just going through the motions. These callers are unprepared, have not done their homework, and act as though they were given a list of names to call and are just checking them off. The caller then reports to some sales manager that the calls were made. The sales manager then reports to some sales/VP that contact was made and the whole 95 percent society lives on. It has often been said, "Nothing happens until someone sells something." In the world of the Ninety-Five Percenters, nothing ever happens.

Only when a salesperson deals with the realities of the marketplace can the person ever thrive in the marketplace. Prospects are, always have been and always will be, inundated with demands for their time and attention. The better salespeople can see what it's like on the other end, the better prepared that person is to be a Five Percenter.

I want to meet, see, and spend time with Five Percenters. These are the people who will help me solve my problems and seize opportunities. Only with the help of the Five Percenters can I begin to think about achieving the goals for my business.

Five Percenters, we need you. Don't let us down!

$$\lambda$$

A program consultant once called me when I was the general manager of the radio station in Houston. The consultant wanted to make an appointment to come see me and discuss the possibility of working with KMJQ. I had never done business with him but knew of him by reputation. KMJQ had an existing relationship with a company that provided research and consulting, but as the new owner, Keymarket wanted to examine every opportunity that might improve the station. The consultant and I set a date and time, and I looked forward to the meeting.

The details of the meeting are not too important. Suffice it to say the presentation was professional and the consultant came across favorably. I was impressed, and we vowed to stay in contact.

As happens on even the best of sales calls, the minute the consultant left my office, I was on to other more pressing and immediate matters and gave the meeting very little additional thought. The gentleman did as he promised and called me to follow up. At first, he called every week to ten days, then ten days to two weeks, then once a month and then less frequently than that. As time went on, I went from taking the calls to getting a message and returning the calls when I had time. The consultant was moving from an A to a B to one of the Cs.

I was busy with the millions of little things that must be attended to in the first six months of operation. Phone calls from the prospective consultant may have been important but not urgent. The company's current consultant was doing a good job. No need to change. No need for additional help.

Reading one of the trade papers one weekend, I took note of a ratings report from a market slightly larger than Houston and a station in a similar format to KMJQ. I read of the station's terrific rating book, and I knew that the consultant who had come to see me worked with the station. I was curious to learn what the consultant had done that helped the station achieve its success. I made a mental note that the next time the consultant called, I would make sure to answer and reopen our talks.

That was twenty-eight years ago. I'm still waiting. The next call never came. Maybe he got too busy and didn't have time for me. Maybe the consultant perceived me to be disinterested. Maybe he grew weary of trying to reach me. I don't know. In addition, he'll never know that my thoughts had shifted.

The point is that clients grow hot and cold. The next call may be the one that gets the client moving. The open window can be narrow and the time short. A prospect may feel an acute urge to act, but that mood can rapidly pass.

When clients do not respond, it may mean something or it may mean nothing. A Five Percenter doesn't get upset trying to figure it out. The Five Percenter stays up, open, and alert for reasons to call. The Five Percenter is ready and available when the client feels the time is right.

I know. No one can be everywhere all the time. So how do the Five Percenters do it?

Five Percenters make more calls . . . more calls on fewer people. The average sale is not made until at least the seventh call, and the average salesperson quits after one to three calls. The Five Percenter knows how to keep the momentum alive through the seventh call to eight, nine, and ten. That's how the Five Percenters do more business. The Five Percenter doesn't call on more prospects. The Five Percenter makes more calls on fewer select prospects. The

Five Percenter goes deep, not wide. This enables the Five Percenter to establish credibility and demonstrate reliability.

The one thing clients worry about most is that their salesperson will make a sale, run off chasing other business, and not follow through. This is a serious concern that, above all other objections, causes most sales to fall apart. A salesperson's repeated and routine calling helps solve this problem and erases the doubt and fear in the prospect's mind.

As the sales process progresses, creating new and interesting reasons for a prospect to be open to seeing a salesperson or take the salesperson's call is a monumental challenge. This is where the salesperson's ability to question, probe, and understand the prospect's situation comes into play. There is no textbook to explain to a salesperson how to do this. The Five Percenter got to where they are by spending days on the street seeing people and learning with every call.

CHAPTER 44

BACKYARD BROADCASTING

Immediately upon the announcement of my departure from Sinclair, I got a call from Barry Baker who had moved from USA Networks to become a partner and managing director at Boston Ventures, the private equity firm that had been a sponsor of River City Broadcasting.

Baker told me BV was looking to invest in the radio space. BV had not had a radio investment since River City sold to Sinclair but liked the fundamental financial characteristics of the business. With the right operator, they would love to get back in. Baker asked me if I had any interest. I didn't have to think about it. Here was a fabulous opportunity for me to get back into radio with partners I knew and trusted.

I started looking at markets and stations, talking with all the brokers and operators I knew, and began to put together ideas on prospective purchases. It was fun using my background, knowledge, and imagination all at the same time.

Over the next year, I visited with many station owners and made several offers, most of which went absolutely nowhere. Many days it looked as if I'd never find a radio deal. I didn't worry about it. A discipline I learned at Keymarket was not to force it. When a deal is lost or falls through, there is always the ability to rebound and get the next one. A bad deal the company has to live with.

Being thoughtful and patient, Boston Ventures and I spent 2002-2004 building Backyard Broadcasting into a group of thirty radio stations in six markets.

The larger markets were already consolidated by the big groups, so we concentrated on the smaller markets 200 plus. Due to the size of the markets, national business was a very small factor. The radio business in the Backyard Broadcasting markets was 95 percent local, and of that, two-thirds done directly with the advertisers and one-third through advertising agencies. Backyard owned excellent technical facilities, and our stations were leaders in each market.

Often I am asked about the name Backyard Broadcasting. All the credit for that goes to my younger brother, the wordsmith of the family. When I was looking for a handle, I called him.

I told him I wanted to go in the opposite direction of everyone else. The media were all claiming to be bigger, masters of the universe, and that being global was better. I wanted a friendly, neighborhood feel.

Also I remembered from my days in Houston, the dominant country station was KIKK, Kick-96FM. When KIKK broadcast the weather, they would give the current temperatures: Houston Intercontinental 76 degrees, Houston Hobby 77 degrees, downtown Houston 79 degrees, and on the back porch at Kick, it's 78 degrees.

"On the back porch" just sounded so warm, friendly, and fun, creating a mental picture of hangin' out sipping iced tea or beer and enjoying the great music together.

So, thank you, Gary Drake for putting it all together for us with the name Backyard Broadcasting.

The very first time I used our name I was calling the top executive of a company in New York. When the executive's secretary asked whom I was with, I said, "Backyard Broadcasting." She literally began to laugh out loud. "It's a hit," I thought to myself.

$$\lambda$$

Having a top-flight executive team was critical to Backyard running a successful operation. Robin Smith from Sinclair joined me as CFO and Tom Atkins as director of engineering. Tom was the chief engineer at the Buffalo radio properties during the Keymarket-River City-Sinclair days. Tom did a magnificent job of turning Backyard's smaller market stations into up-to-date and efficient technical plants.

Cathy Donaldson, another Sinclair veteran and a whiz at financial reporting systems became Backyard's corporate controller. I brought in Shane Media
to work with the station program directors on music, programming, and
promotions.

Backyard Broadcasting had a fine group of market managers: Dan Farr in
Williamsport, Smitty O'Loughlin in Corning-Elmira, John Morton in Olean,
Bruce Law, and later Amy Dillon, in Muncie, Indiana, Craig Hodgson in Sioux
Falls, and Marshall Magee and later Curt Peterson in Mississippi. All believed
in playing an active and vital role in their communities and maintaining strong
relationships with the top decision makers of our local advertisers.

А

With Backyard Broadcasting, I was back into the routine of being in each market for a day or two every four to six weeks, working with the managers and
the salespeople, and spending time with our top advertisers. We brought in
Philip LeNoble and his successor, Michael Guld, with System 21 and dedicated
Backyard's sales effort to building a solid foundation with long-term local direct
business. Backyard Broadcasting's concentration on client-oriented presentations and strong commercial copy helped keep our eyes on the ball as more stories were being circulated in the media trades about radio's challenges in the new
world of satellites, iPods, iTunes, and the Internet. At Backyard, we understood
and acknowledged the existence of this new technology but, by staying close to
our customers and remaining focused on their results, we were not affected.

In early 2004, Pepsi came to us in one of the markets. As part of their radio
buy, they wanted the station to run an on-air contest giving away iPods (provided
by Pepsi). Our program director had a fit. "I refuse," he screamed. "I will not
encourage my listeners to use iPods. Why should I send listeners to iPods when
I want them with me on the radio station?" I helped him understand. "We can't
stick our heads in the sand and pretend these gadgets don't exist," I told him.
"In fact, we want to be a part of the culture with our listeners." I took him back
to a time before he was born. "We had a thing when I was a kid called a record
player. We loaded it (using a more modern term) with 45s, singles, and played the
records repeatedly. But we knew which records we liked and wanted to buy from

hearing them on the radio. The record player actually made us use radio more." I didn't bore him with stories of how many records we used to give away on radio stations and listeners waiting to call in and win the new Bee Gees album. I believed what I said that day. It wasn't just to get the buy, although I was glad to please Pepsi.

What I learned from talking directly with business people is they don't care about any of these new inventions. Business owners and managers care about themselves and their businesses. When a technological development comes along, and the new device can be used to improve business, advertisers are happy to use it. These same clients, however, are just as happy staying with the suppliers they trust to perform. The key for radio salespeople is not to pooh-pooh new media options. The key is to demonstrate how radio is working.

If the demonstration only involves ratings against other radio, "KB-104 has a 4.1 with women 35-49," the salesperson is going to have a tough time. Yet when a radio salesperson demonstrates the radio station's track record of success in generating response, the station will remain not only relevant but also highly desirable to the advertiser.

I remember again the voice of Paul Rothfuss from the 1970s, "Make sure something happens in the store when the commercials run on the air." It is critical to design the commercial copy to elicit an immediate response from the listeners. The client wants to feel something good the second the commercial campaign starts on the air.

⅄

The combined effect of client benefit proposals and effective copy created demand, and the success of the campaigns led to a scarcity of commercial inventory. This enabled the stations to grow rates. The rates had to grow in order to grow revenue. Adding commercial units was not an option. Backyard maintained that pricing was always fair; fair to the clients because they were seeing a return on investment, and fair to the stations because it permitted the stations to continue to provide good service.

When music fans want to see the sold out George Strait Cowboy Rides Away show at the Staple Center, they pay whatever the price is. If they want to see

Bruno Mars sing live at the half-time show, they buy a ticket. The quality of service and performance dictate the fair price.

⟡

The Backyard Broadcasting market managers also devoted a good deal of time to recruiting and interviewing salespeople. At the annual company budget meetings, the managers and I would come up with goals each year for hiring one or two more salespeople than existing station revenue dictated. There are many reasons for building and keeping a larger sales staff. I will zero in on just four:

1. Regardless of how many salespeople are on staff today and no matter how good and experienced they are, hundreds of prospects remain in the market who are not being called on and will never be seen. More salespeople mean more contacts.

2. Someone on the staff is going to resign this week. If someone doesn't resign this week, someone is thinking about it and will continue to think about it next week. If not that, someone on the staff is sick or getting sick, and will need some time off. Or someone has a relative or friend to care for and will be less than 100 percent effective for a time. More salespeople equal better backup.

3. The current salespeople, the experienced ones, the stars, must constantly motivate themselves to perform. It is easier for salespeople to stay highly motivated when someone is nipping at their heels. More salespeople provide this stimulus.

   a. Stars love to perform, to show off. The stars must have an audience for whom to perform. The rookie salespeople provide a gallery.

4. More salespeople mean more competition for the station's commercial avails.

⟡

I don't know who said it first, maybe one of those Chinese military geniuses in 500 BC, but I like the phrase so much I used it all the time: "Manage the Accounts. Lead the Salespeople."

People are to be worked with. People are to be led. Accounts can be managed. Manage the account lists. The accounts belong to the station, to the company. It is the duty and responsibility of the company leadership to manage the accounts. The company decides who is best to call on each account. Regardless of title, GSM, LSM, SM, DOS, or GM, the number one priority of sales management is managing the accounts and account lists. Numerous tools are available to help with this, sophisticated computer programs to good old paper and pencil. It doesn't make a difference what tool is used. Pick one and do it.

Keymarket's sales manager in Austin was exceptional at this. Marcy faithfully conducted a one-on-one meeting with each salesperson every week. At the meeting, Marcy had in front of her the salesperson's plan from the prior week, their plan for the upcoming week, and a printout of the salesperson's account list. Marcy and the salesperson would go through the names on the account list and look at the two weekly planners. When an account name came up and that account did not appear on either of the two planners, Marcy would say, "Well, I guess we can remove that account from your list."

What a simple way to let the salesperson know what is expected and unless there is work on the account, it can't sit on the list.

When management does its job of managing the accounts, leading the salespeople will come naturally. With thorough account management, the salespeople know they are responsible for action and attention to the businesses on their lists.

CHAPTER 45

TIME OUT

Special Report #6: Juggling

Form a mental picture of a playground. There are two kids on a seesaw. When one goes up, the other goes down. Got the picture?

As I rode with Backyard salespeople, I began to see how the seesaw was affecting performance. This was not a new phenomenon. It only became more pronounced the past few years.

In prehistoric times, it was an AM salesperson given an FM to sell. One station would gain while the other suffered. When salespeople were given multiple products or projects to sell, print pieces, sweepstakes giveaways, booths at an expo, one item on the call would get attention and all else would drop. The principle affects the clients, too. When the client became engaged in one product, it would preclude the client's interest in others. Just human nature.

When ownership loaded additional stations onto the plates of station salespeople, the problem magnified.

Salespeople figure out for themselves what they are best able to sell and what is most profitable for them. When a salesperson decides a promotion is too hard to explain or they just don't understand it, the salesperson will drop it. If a salesperson likes a promotion and sees it as a get-money-quick idea that will almost sell itself, they'll push it, but this comes at the expense of any long-term selling. Seesaw. One goes up. The other goes down. When responsible for selling a group of stations, the "cluster," salespeople will generally find one or two stations they are confident in selling, stick with those, and the rest go unsold.

Meanwhile back at the office or in the corporate womb, management deludes itself into believing all ships will rise. The day-to-day long-term base business will occur on each of the stations, and simultaneously, the add-ons, the extras, the specials, and the corporate initiatives will all sell too. Not likely.

Now I know this may sound as though I am being critical of the abilities and work ethic of the salespeople. Not at all. I am simply reporting what I have witnessed over forty years and forty thousand calls from all sides: salesperson, sales management, and client. The 2013 report from the Center for Sales Strategy, CSS, provides additional evidence. The study shows the disparity between the priorities of management and the priorities of the salespeople.

CHAPTER 46

AND AGAIN

During my forty years, the United States has seen five recessions. The economists will tell you there have been six, but the forty thousand calls I made tell me that five is the right number. The short recession in 1980 is counted as a separate recession by the economists, but to those in business at the time, it was part of the longer 1981-1982 recession. Like everyone else, I went through these five recessions. I had a bonus with the oil patch recession in the mid-1980s.

Recessions are simply part of life. They come and they go. Only two things are for sure:

1. There will always be another recession.
2. At some point, every recession will end.

Recessions and expansions are the ying and the yang of the economy. It is the economy breathing, inhaling and exhaling. After a period of expansion, it breathes out for a while. When it needs oxygen, it grows again. Consumers are most often given the credit, and rightfully so, of ending recessions. After a period of holding back, there is a pent-up demand that causes a flurry of spending and the economy grows. Witness 2013's new car sales. After hitting a low of 10 million in 2009, sales increased four years in a row and now are heading back to the 2007 level of 16 million per year.

I would love to say Backyard Broadcasting was prepared for the financial crisis that hit in September of 2008 and the Great Recession that followed. No one was completely prepared for the severity of this downturn, but I can share what the company did know and what Backyard was able to do at that time.

The early warning signs appeared in the summer of 2007. Again, the accounts receivable gave the first heads-up. Clients began to delay payments. The thirty-day guys turned into sixty, and the sixties into ninety. In the third week of September 2007, I saw fourth quarter bookings stall. That same week, Target Stores warned of lower traffic counts in its stores. Trouble was on the horizon.

Midyear-2008 revenue at Backyard Broadcasting was up over midyear 2007, but the gains were due to national and the local/regional agency business. The base of local direct was down. I knew total revenue was headed for a decline. It was time for action.

The station managers worked with the salespeople using two tools: a wonderful book by Jeffrey Fox, *How to Become a Rainmaker*, and Paul Weyland's *Direct Selling Step by Step* audio disc. Each of these programs concentrates on the customer's wants and the station's and salesperson's accountability. The message to the salespeople was to "keep moving and do good work." The economic headwinds would be strong, we relayed, but we'd be all right as long as we adhered to the guidelines taught by Jeffery and Paul.

Normally, as recovery gets underway, the advertising business returns to prior levels quickly. This wasn't going to be normal. I had to prepare the salespeople for something different. I said, "This economic downturn uniquely coincides with a dramatic emergence of new technology. While we are navigating through this recession, the smartphone is becoming a staple and Internet advertising will come of age." So not only were the managers and I guiding the sales effort through the recession, but also readying ourselves for the new world.

↟

As Backyard Broadcasting operated through the storm of 2009, the ship was battered but the damage was minimal in comparison to the radio industry at large. The fact that the company owned dominant positions in its markets, forged close relationships with the major decision makers of the top clients, and had salespeople who understood the value of being responsible for results led Backyard through this most difficult year.

As the company moved into 2010-2011, we renewed our efforts with System 21 to help the advertisers better plan for the new realities of the marketplace. By mid-2012, the headwind was a tailwind. The hard and thoughtful work was paying off. I was never as proud of a group as I was of Backyard Broadcasting.

⋏

Experiencing extreme danger and avoiding calamity always has an effect on investors. I saw this when we worked our way through the 1990-91 recession at Keymarket. When the clouds part and there is the hint of blue sky, there is such relief that investors count their blessings, and their money, too. By 2012, it was time for Boston Ventures to exit the Backyard Broadcasting investment.

As Backyard Broadcasting carried out the process of divesting, I worked hand in hand with Kalil and Company to find good homes for the radio stations and our people. I was very pleased to see the Backyard stations go to solid, dedicated radio broadcasters committed to compelling programming, effective sales, and strong ties to the community.

PART SIX
RADIO TODAY AND TOMORROW

CHAPTER 47

SOS: State of the Stations

After forty years and forty thousand sales calls, I have some opinions on where the radio business is today and where it is headed, as well as some ideas on what could happen, and perhaps should happen. I'll begin with a look at where radio is right now statistically, how advertisers are voting with their dollars. Here is a look at the radio industry's current revenue picture and likely direction of revenue over most of the next decade.

The Radio Advertising Bureau reported radio revenue for 2013 of $17.649 billion, a 0.4 percent gain over 2012. Since 2012 was a big political year, it is best to compare 2013 with 2011 when revenue was $17.4 billion. The year 2013 gained 1.5 percent over 2011.

The good news is there was a gain. The bad news is a gain of less than 1 percent a year cannot support the natural rise in operating expenses, not to mention capital expenses and any debt service. That is to say, with revenue going up less than 1 percent, just to maintain the bottom line expenses must be slashed. This does not bode well for the future.

The big story from RAB and radio company executives is the 2013 gain of 16 percent in digital revenue. But this means that core radio revenue declined 1 percent compared to 2012 and showed no gain over 2011.

Radio revenue peaked in 2006 at $21.7 billion. Using 2013's revenue as a base, even if core radio revenue were to remain flat and digital revenue could continue to grow 16 percent per year (and assuming network and other off-air revenues grow at 5 percent each year), it will take another eight years, 2022, to reach the revenue of 2006.

But this scenario shows a total revenue growth rate of less than 3 percent per year and in the first three years of this eight-year span, less than 2 percent. Unless a company is able to withstand negative growth in operating income, expenses will have to be reduced. With further reductions in service and personnel, how realistic is it to assume core radio revenue can remain flat?

The softness of the core radio advertising is troubling. It puts the entire industry in jeopardy. And what about this growth in digital that is talked about so much?

RAB began reporting digital revenue in 2009, at $480 million: 3 percent of the total revenue. Today, digital is reported to be $889 million, or 5 percent of the total. The projections above show 2022 digital at $3.4 billion and 16 percent of total revenue.

ᴧ

But is the digital revenue being reported, the $889 million, real or fictitious? That is, is it additional revenue? Or is it simply a reallocation of revenue that would have otherwise been recorded as core radio revenue?

Based on the advertisers I have spoken with over the past two years, clients as well as advertising agencies, the answer is yes.

When discussing the subject with a digital agency or a small client without the means for a radio budget, the dollars invested in digital are specific digital revenues.

On the other hand, most regular radio advertisers expect to get digital products offered by radio stations free. These radio advertisers couldn't care less how the station wants to show and bill the revenue.

Does it matter if revenues are reported as radio revenue, digital revenue, or just total revenue? I ask the question for one reason.

The issue of revenue growth can only be addressed when there is an honest assessment of where the business currently is, an assessment that shows what resources are being invested to produce the current revenue and what the necessities are for growth. In order to develop a course of action for the future, the current situation must be accurately determined. And that starts with honesty.

Radio stations have been offering products additional to commercials since the beginning of time. "Buy a schedule-get a jingle. Buy a jingle-get a schedule. Buy a schedule-we'll include you in our fall promotion. Buy an ad in my fall circular-get a schedule of commercials to support it. As part of your annual buy, you'll have a coupon on the back of my bumper sticker. Make a big annual buy, and I'll put you on the front of my bumper sticker!"

How this revenue was accounted for varied by station and by advertiser and varied case-by-case. Was it all radio or should it be recorded in "other?" Usually it just came down to preference. Some clients would want it split a certain way, and stations did their best to keep the client happy.

As radio got to the mid to late 1990s, many of these inducements moved to website promotions. This served to create content for the new sites, give advertisers an Internet presence, and slash the costs of all the printing associated with many of radio's value-added offerings.

The point being, radio stations had digital revenue for ten to fifteen years before it was broken out into a separate line in the RAB report. Where was digital revenue reported before 2009? Some of it was on the radio (core) revenue line and some in the category named "off-air," which was a combination of revenues from events, ticket sales, T-shirt sales, and other promotions, print pieces, etc.

Trying to get a handle on this is made especially difficult as the first year of digital reporting was 2009, the same year core radio revenue declined $3.2 billion as a result of the Great Recession. Was some of the decline because digital was moved from radio to its own line at $480 million? How about the off-air line? It went from $1.8 billion in 2008 to $1.3 billion in 2009 (a convenient difference of $500 million). All that is known for sure is that there was digital revenue before 2009, but now it had a line of its own.

⚔

Since 2009, the digital revenue line reported by RAB has grown from $480 million to $889 million, a gain of 85 percent, identical to the growth rate of Internet advertising in the United States. In 2009, the Interactive Advertising Bureau said revenue was $23 billion, and in 2013, it was $42.8 billion, 85 percent growth. From 2009 to 2013, the share of online advertising sold by radio stations remained the same, 2 percent. Is it possible that the share of online revenue sold by radio stations can grow? Should radio stations even attempt to grow share? And, if so, how?

Here are two ways to approach the question.

Back in my days at Feller's Men's store a rack was positioned on the way to the cash register. The rack stood about four feet high and six feet wide and on the shelves were white T-shirts and briefs: underwear. Since no one ever came in to buy underwear, I asked our manager why the store carried it. The manager explained that it was important to carry underwear as a convenience to the store's customers. When a man came in and bought two suits and a blazer, the store always wanted to have shirts and ties to sell along with the suits and offered underwear so that the customer wouldn't have to be bothered going someplace else. Underwear was stocked as a courtesy to the store's customers. No expectation existed that anyone would come in looking to buy underwear. The store was in the clothing business and that's where the money was. Underwear was a convenience item. No concerted effort was made to improve the underwear revenue line.

$$\curlywedge$$

Here is the opposite approach.

One of America's most prominent retailers is The Limited. They sell skirts, sweaters, tops, shorts, and dresses for women. A little over thirty years ago, The Limited decided to expand into the up-and-coming category of ladies luxury lingerie, aka underwear.

What The Limited Did Not Do:

The Limited did not buy some fashion underwear to put on the Limited Stores' shelves and command The Limited sales clerks to sell underwear to The Limited customers. The Limited knew this kind of selling would be to the detriment of the skirts and dresses and sweaters and shorts and slacks and blouses.

What The Limited Did:

The Limited bought a small upstart in San Francisco, Victoria's Secret. The Limited built Victoria's Secret stores nationwide, hired salespeople for these stores, and trained them specifically in the art of selling underwear.

Two very distinct approaches and analogous to the situation today in radio.

⋏

At the RAIN Conference earlier this year, I heard a panelist make total sense as he described the digital products at his radio station. He said these programming and promotional tools are a means to enhance the relationship between the listener and the station or the station's personalities. With that in mind, he explained these digital products could be made available to advertisers, too, in order to embellish their radio commercial campaign. The digital product is an add-on, an extra (underwear) NOT the lead item. The salespeople offered the station's digital products: video, SEO, display, social, email supplements, etc., as a convenience, an add-on to the radio campaigns of existing customers.

Unless a radio station is willing and able to invest the time and resources into building a "Victoria's Secret" for digital business, a separate business with separate budgets, staff, and structure, then digital must remain the underwear rack, the convenience add-on. I am not claiming one is right and the other wrong, only that station ownership must make a decision. Otherwise, having the radio salespeople focus on selling digital products as anything more than an add-on will only damage the efforts to grow radio revenue. The core radio product, commercial campaigns, will continue to suffer.

Just recently, I saw an interview with the manager of radio stations in a significant market who said his salespeople were having difficulty getting appointments with prospects to sell radio. Now the salespeople are calling prospects to make appointments to sell digital. According to the manager, the prospective clients are so intrigued by the Internet that it is easier to get appointments this way and then maybe get them interested in radio. The interviewer asked, "So you get appointments for online advertising and then try to work radio in later?" The manager bellowed, "Yes, that's right, you've got it."

Sorry, folks. I ain't buyin' it. I'm not buying this approach, because this will only confuse the clients and distract them from what they are really looking for.

Yes, business people are curious about digital. But what do these prospects really want? Response. Action. Results!

Interest and appointments are aroused by the salesperson demonstrating the radio station's ability to deliver a return, not with a trick to gain access with some new gimmick or toy. If radio is to grow revenue, radio must have the confidence to lead with its strengths, delivering demonstrable results through the execution of commercial campaigns.

Winners know their strengths and play the game accordingly. Winners stay on top of the competition by playing their game, not by being more like the other guy. Would Peyton Manning play a football game and not throw a pass? A winner stands tall and says, "I know my strength, you know my strength. I'm coming at you. Let's see if you can stop me."

There is tremendous appeal to efficiency-minded business people to run small ads, try to engage in social, and send emails to current customers. This can help retain customers. But eventually every customer goes away. Customers move, their needs change, they are enticed to go elsewhere, and they die. The obsession with mining the same database brings in revenue at an attractive ROI, for a while. As the cycle runs through, the business will contract. For a business to sustain itself and grow it must find new customers; it must expand the market. This may not be efficient. There will be waste. But what is the alternative? Shrinking and withering away?

A few months ago while out on the road with a salesperson, I sat with one of Backyard Broadcasting's automotive advertisers. The dealer talked about what the Internet has meant to his store's business. He related how customers are more knowledgeable now when coming into the showroom about the car they want and the price they want to pay, and how the store's salespeople have to be ready to deal with customers on a different level than in the past. The dealer went on to say how this makes advertising even more important. And he was quick to add, "Some little two-inch banner or pop-up on a computer screen or some one-line thing on a telephone isn't really advertising. It's OK," he continued, "but when I say advertising, I mean BIG: MAKING A SPLASH—Big ads to dominate the page in the paper or frequency to dominate the day(s) on radio. Advertising to get attention, get people excited, and get them in here. And radio," the dealer finished, "radio has what no one else has. That immediate call to action."

It was the best radio pitch I heard all day!

The unique value of the medium of radio is that a radio campaign can do it all. Radio talks to the clients' customers, present, past, and future. Radio can build the brand, create a market, and call buyers to action . . . all at the same time. And radio has been doing it all for almost 100 years!

CHAPTER 48

SOS, Part Two

Having sized up the State of the Stations statistically, here is a more conceptual analysis based on a few questions I am frequently asked.

What about streaming? Who sells the commercials on the station's stream?
If the radio station has one staff for selling on-air and the stream, then the station must either run no commercials on the stream or simulcast the on-air sound 100 percent and duplicate the commercials. Yes, an extra charge can be added if possible but that again gets into revenue allocation.

It is not in the station's best interest to have the existing sales staff, the people responsible for the station's largest volume advertisers, selling tiny advertisers online inventory for pennies. If a radio station wants to generate a new and separate advertiser base for the stream, then the station must hire separate salespeople to do it.

What about the online services? Should radio operators be concerned about these?
Yes. Radio programmers must always be on guard and prepared to fight for the attention and time of the audience.

Last year I attended a conference where one of the presenters was Tom Conrad of Pandora. After the meeting, he and I talked for a few minutes, and he asked me if, as a traditional radio station operator, I was concerned about Pandora. I said, "Yes, of course I am. I look at Pandora the same as I do *Wheel of Fortune*. If my listener goes away to watch *Wheel*, I had better have a reason for that listener to come back to my station. If my listener goes away to listen to Pandora? Same thing." The fact is that listeners are always coming and going. The radio programmer's job is to get listeners to come more than they go. Realize that from time to time even the most faithful listeners will go. The station must have content that will bring the listeners back.

What about on the sales side? Will Pandora salespeople cut into the radio budget?

Sure they will. The same way Comcast and Time Warner cable have. The advertising pie must be viewed as a whole. The other night I spoke with the owner of a furniture store. He told me he was using outdoor this year for the first time. This guy has been in business for forty years, and he's using an old medium for the very first time. He said, "I just thought I'd give this a whirl." Advertisers wake up every morning looking for some way to get a jump on the market and improve business. Radio's challenge is not the other radio group in town, or digital, or mobile. It is *all of the above.*

What about iHeart?

Some clients are beginning to notice iHeart. Not so much for what it is, an app for music and radio listening, as for what it does—the festival in Las Vegas, the holiday concerts, and the awards show on TV. The clients who like being sponsors, having signage at the venue and a few tickets to the shows, realize the value creation is on the backs of the radio stations. Without the radio stations there is nothing.

ᛝ

This brings me to the question I am still often asked, some fifteen years after leaving TV. "What did you see as the difference between television and radio?"

First, the similarities. Television and radio have identical objectives in attempting to attract, build, and hold an audience. It's the reason Bill Paley was able to seamlessly transition CBS programming leadership from radio to television in the 1940s and 1950s. Paley already knew the qualities necessary to please an audience. It was just a matter of transferring to the new medium. The process and the content changed somewhat going from audio to audio/video, but the basic idea was the same. Some say that new methods of distribution and delivery will affect the creative content of shows. I agree more with what actor Kevin Spacey had to say after doing *House of Cards* for Netflix, "That camera doesn't know if it's a film camera or a TV camera or a streaming camera. It's just a camera." It's the content, not the delivery mechanism, that's important. As in radio, television must work to be sure the programs are interesting, the news is accurate and credible, the personalities engaging and reliable.

The biggest difference I noticed between the day-to-day operation of a television station and a radio station is that in television, management and salespeople refer to programming as "it." *Friends*? It did a 6! *Judge Joe Brown*? It did a 2! The *10 O'clock News*? It did a 5 last night!

Every business has its customs, and calling programming "it" is one of those in television. The word *it* stems, however, from the fact that the programming on television comes primarily from outside sources, a network or a TV production company studio, unlike in radio where the salespeople personally know the on-air performers, the morning team, the sports guy. The salespeople see the on-air staffers, work with them, and are members of the same community. In radio, the salespeople don't call the morning show "it," they say "Tom, Cathy, and Steve."

Television stations have their anchors, reporters, and personalities but management puts a Chinese wall between news and the sales staff. So the news programming remains "it" too.

I believe the alliance of sales and programming inside radio stations is the biggest advantage radio has over television on the street. Radio is live and the personalities are local, and this is not just a selling point in itself but contains practical applications when using the talent properly to do commercials and appearances. Advertisers see the benefit of their association with popular personalities.

For the time being, on the local level, radio holds an advantage over television, although that advantage is in danger of being washed away. While television stations are working to expand their live hours, radio promotes an ever-increasing number of network shows.

CHAPTER 49

RADIO'S FUTURE

These are not predictions but my opinions, based on forty years and forty thousand sales calls on advertisers. Because there is no "one" radio customer, I have put the advertisers into six general groups.

1. Local direct accounts
2. Local/regional accounts and agencies
3. Network accounts
4. National accounts
5. Radio's big clients
6. Big clients with big agencies, often multiple agencies. The biggest advertising spenders in the United States

Local Direct
In the fall of 2010 at the NAB Radio Show in Washington, one of the sessions was titled "Retailers in Radio." I went to the session in spite of being disappointed only one retailer appeared on the panel: Ron Mervis of Mervis Diamond Importers, a three-store jeweler in the metropolitan DC market. The other members of the panel were two middle managers from the client side and a lady from an advertising agency.

When the panel was questioned about how they determined the effectiveness of their campaigns, the three nonretailers went into long descriptions of their computer models and the data they review. When Ron Mervis began to answer (he was last to go) he apologized for his lack of sophistication but said his system worked for him. Ron explained how his office was on the store's second floor. When he got up from his desk, he would turn around and look out his window that overlooked the store's parking lot. "When the parking lot is full," Ron said, "I know the campaign is working."

Local direct advertisers feel, hear, and see the value of radio every day. When radio salespeople call on advertisers properly, i.e., determine what they want and devise a plan to deliver it, the clients love it. This will not change. The key is working properly, taking the time to get to the wants of the decision maker, and delivering. In doing so, the salesperson takes charge of the creative, and that is what triggers the effect. In markets 100 plus, local direct business runs 60-70 percent of a station's total revenue. That percentage declines as market size goes up, but local direct is very important in all but the largest markets. The relationships radio stations have with direct advertisers will remain healthy and positive because radio stations will continue to produce the tangible and measurable results clients desire.

Local/Regional Accounts and Agencies

In markets of all sizes, this group is crucial. It is a large volume of business and very diverse. It includes most of the auto dealer business, larger retail, grocery, financial, and telecom. The success a station has in securing business from clients in this group may not be 100 percent ratings driven, but ratings play a big part. This group is fragile. It is fragile because many stations treat it passively or, at best, semi-actively. Some stations handle it as they do national; when there is an avail, they negotiate the best deal possible. If the station's ratings are consistently strong and show a decided advantage over the radio competition (and how many stations can say that?) business may be OK. But just maybe. Because in this group the competition isn't other radio, or even the poorly sold and now declining newspaper, but video.

I don't say television, cable, or even the Internet because that is media selection and not of serious concern at the agency. Producing video is what matters. Where the video runs, if the video runs, does not matter. The agency mission is to get the client committed to writing checks for video production.

Once a client starts down the video road, radio stations are in big trouble. There may be NO budget for radio, or "we'll still use you for store openings and our once-a-year Founders Celebration" or "we are going to consider radio for special opportunities."

I am not describing a new problem, but it becomes larger every year because total ad spend is being scrutinized more and more due to the challenges of the no-growth United States economy. Agencies can only spend what clients are willing to invest; with budgets being held flat year after year, less and less exists to go around. Logically, the agency puts the squeeze on the radio budget. At the same time, radio is getting less and less face time at the agency. Smaller sales staffs and fewer salespeople selling more stations mean less influence for radio at the agency. The foolish notion of letting regional telephone call centers attempt to sell radio advertising is not even worthy of comment.

Unlike the local direct advertiser, the advertiser with a local/regional agency is removed from the process. At one time, these businesses may have been local direct but have grown in either sales volume or geographic scope and have determined the need for the assistance of advertising professionals. When radio stations relinquish the responsibility for selling these businesses and turn that duty over to the agency, a third party, it spells trouble for radio.

Network and Barter

What do these accounts think of radio? If they think about radio at all, it can be summed up in one word: cheap. Agencies like network because a network buy is such a simple transaction. So when Geico hands over a $1.2 billion advertising budget, throwing a few bucks on network radio is no big deal. What about the future? What about the moves being made by radio's largest companies to bring radio back to the 1940s? The days of network programming to local affiliates? Will this not create more emphasis on network business? Will network revenue grow? Sure it will, at the expense of national.

I used to see this happen in television all the time. The network sales division eyes an account buying national spot. The pitch to the agency goes like this: "Why go to all the time and trouble to buy each individual market when with just one buy, you can have the entire country?" And when the agency rebuts with "but our client doesn't have outlets in every market." The network seller says, "So what. So you get exposure in markets where you have yet to have stores. It's not as if you have to pay for these markets. Your total cost on a network buy will be lower than your spot buy with a lot less work. We take care of the placement, the invoicing, and the authorization of payment." Case closed. The radio networks will grow by cannibalizing national.

National

The national rep has always served two masters: the station and the agency. The stations have taken the backseat (they may even be in the trunk). When I was in the rep business back in the Stone Age, at least fifteen different rep firms fought to prove themselves to their station clients. The station client contracts had ninety-day outs. The rep had to perform every day. I feel the pain of the good people at the firm who spend their days explaining to the stations how buys went down in the midst of the firm's internal conflicts of interest. The time of rep competitiveness and national selling is over, so I'll continue from the advertiser's viewpoint.

An advertiser is designated national, not because the business advertises in all parts of the nation, although it might, but because the agency the business employs is geographically located in one of the dozen or so cities or territories where rep firms have offices. So when looking at national business, these are clients not unlike those in the local/regional agency category. It's up to the agency to sell the client on using radio. How likely is that?

Exceptions exist. I know a few stories circulate every year about a business deciding radio is the way to go. Bonefish Restaurants comes to mind. I know there is an idea presented every now and then by an agency account executive to a media manager or marketing director at the client level that results in some revenue for radio. But as a rule? No.

Radio's Big Accounts

This is the 80-20 rule in action. There are a dozen or so accounts on every station that are the Big Ones. These businesses may represent only 5 percent of the accounts on the air, but can represent 30-35 percent of the month's revenue.

Some of these Big Ones are national, some are local agency, and a few are direct. Each of the Big Ones must be worked as though they are direct. These businesses are so important that constant contact must continue between the station and the client. Every salesperson knows the problem here. When one of these accounts drops off, takes a hiatus, or when expenditures decline even just a little, it is maddening to add enough new business in the short run to make up the difference. Stations are always susceptible here. For radio's core revenue to grow, constant contact with these accounts is vital.

The Big Clients—The Really Big Ones with Big Agencies or Multiple Agencies

These are the biggest ad spenders in the United States, including AT&T, McDonald's, Gieco, Macy's, and Wal-Mart, just to name a few. How is radio doing with these accounts? Are these accounts on radio?

Sure they are. But at what level? At what percentage of the total budget? And at what rates (especially for those on the air through the networks)?

It is widely reported that radio is to become a part of the media models the agencies use. This is being promoted as a real boost to the potential for increased radio spending. I agree that being a part of the model must be better than not being a part of the model, but to say it will move spending levels up? Why should that be assumed? There will still be the priority at the agency to shoot video. A second priority is to continue education through experimentation in digital.

The agencies are learning the online business through trial and error. Their clients foot the bill. The same thing happened when TV arrived in the 1950s. At that time, the largest media were print: newspapers and magazines. The agencies had to learn the new medium of television, so it became a part of the proposal to the client. The agencies received an all-expense-paid education on producing and placing television. Now this is happening with digital. Radio being in the media models is not likely to cause agencies to deviate from pursuing their top priorities.

Tied to this is programmatic, automated, or mechanical buying. Put the buying criteria into a computer program and let the machine do the work. No need for salespeople telling a story to influence decision making. "Have your machine call my machine, do the deal, and run the commercials." Radio stations can eliminate reps and agencies can eliminate buyers, a bottom line boost for everyone. But I see all this as a sideshow.

⚓

Radio's challenge with the Big Clients at the Big Agencies runs deeper. Earlier I covered the issue of radio's expanded commercialization that started in the mid to late 1990s. It's a real problem. With no limits on inventory, the supply and demand curve does not exist, and there's no chance for pricing progress. No pricing progress, no revenue growth.

While driving into New York City on a Thursday afternoon in the summer of 2011 and consuming AM/FM radio like only a radio person can, changing stations every few seconds in order to hear every commercial and station promotional announcement, it hit me. These stations are busy. The commercial breaks are loaded. How in the world is radio revenue just limping along flat when these major stations are filled with commercials?

Driving through Orlando last Thursday, listening to a station that is well rated and highly ranked with adults in midday, I counted seventeen commercials in one hour, one of the two breaks carried ten commercials. Is radio trapped in a downward spiral? Stations price for share and lower the rates, and then add units to make budget. Adding units hurts time spent listening and the rating points drop, which means that the rates will drop, which means the unit count goes up and. . . . For radio to grow, there must be rate increases, which can only come from attention to the inventory issue.

Early in 2013, the announcement from FOX that the commercial inventory in the Super Bowl was sold out was no big news. What got my attention was the 5 percent rate increase over the prior year. And the 42 percent increase over the last ten years. These increases were granted by the same advertising agencies that over the same period have commanded radio stations hold rates flat or even reduce rates to get a buy.

How is it these same ad execs can justify increases of 5 percent over last year and 42 percent over the past ten years? Maybe it's because the client, the advertiser, said, "I want it."

When I say *client*, when I say *advertiser*, I am not referring to marketing people and media people. I am talking about the real client, the person responsible for the business, the BOSS.

⋏

Every organization, every business has one. The BOSS. The top person who sets the tone, gives the direction, and calls the shots. There may be a board of directors, an executive committee, numerous task forces, and special panels, but there is only one BOSS. It doesn't matter if the business is a tire and battery store in Magee, Mississippi, or a global manufacturing company with division presidents in seven countries, there is one BOSS. When the BOSS says left, everyone moves left. When the BOSS says I want green, that's the color ordered. Sometimes the BOSS doesn't even have to go that far. The BOSS can just ask, "Did you ever think of green?" And boom. The color is green. The BOSS makes the call, gives the order. Only when a salesperson is talking with the BOSS, is the salesperson really in the game. Of course, plenty of business is transacted between middle managers and the subordinates every day. These transactions add up to a lot of money for radio stations, $17 billion last year. But where does the other $370 billion in advertising spend go? Ask the BOSS!

It can be argued that getting to the BOSS at the tire and battery store in Magee is relatively easy, but the head of an international company? Be serious.

Getting to the BOSS of a large company can be more difficult. Difficult, not impossible. Once a salesperson or station manager makes up their mind to see the BOSS, many methods and techniques can be used, many paths taken. (Because each situation is different, and calls for its own strategy—and respecting the confidentiality of the relationships I have with station managers I have worked with—I won't get into the specific moves here.) Does every attempt work every time? Surely not. When an attempt does work, though, it changes the game. Then the radio station or the salesperson is in a position to exert influence on the one person who can really make a difference, really give a boost to revenue, the BOSS.

Always remember the BOSS is a person too. The BOSS has the same basic concerns as everyone else. Is my spouse happy? Are my kids on the right track?

Should I buy a new plane? (OK, some of their concerns may be a little different, but it's all relative.) And when it comes to business, the BOSS always needs help. Because after all, with whom does the BOSS talk? Other BOSSES, who only know the same things and have the same concerns. The BOSS has a tough time getting the people who work in his business to open up and speak, so the BOSS works a good deal in the dark. The BOSS craves outside input. But who calls?

When someone does call, and is persistent enough to get through multiple gatekeepers and the scheduling obstructions of a busy executive, the BOSS will still be wary. The BOSS must ask, "Who is this person? Are they serious? Are they time wasters? Are they spies?"

Being dedicated to making calls of this caliber is on the one hand frustrating due to the time and effort that must be put forth. On the other hand, one never feels more energized, more relevant, and more important than when spending time with a BOSS.

Wait a minute, "Don't the BOSSES at big companies have agencies? Don't radio stations have to worry about the agency? What about that?" Legitimate questions.

Well, here's another good question, "Don't agencies get fired?" Yes, it happens every week. Agencies sell the idea that they are wed to the client forever and always and then wham, the news is out the client has called for an agency review or makes a switch with no warning at all.

Unless the head of the agency and the BOSS were frat brothers, sorority sisters, or the agency head is the BOSS'S son-in-law, one thing is certain: the agency's days are numbered. Every advertising agency business plan states this principle: The agency starts losing a client the day the agency signs the client. That's why all the rewards and bonuses at agencies go to the people who bring in the new accounts. The business plan calls for each account to expire. Every agency calculates the average life of an account like an actuary, so feeding the pipeline is job one.

The BOSS looks at the agency as another vendor. I don't intend to sound demeaning or to offend. Agencies do important work and provide essential services but are employees of the BOSS. The BOSS hires—or approves of hiring—vendors to carry out certain functions or to perform tasks that the company doesn't want to do in-house. A fast food chain doesn't farm its own wheat. It buys buns from a bread company. An auto parts chain doesn't produce commercials and buy media. It hires an advertising agency.

⚔

About ten years ago, a big agency called to place an order on one of our radio stations through the national rep firm for a large company doing business in every city in America. Unfortunately, the station general manager had to decline the order because the advertiser was months in arrears. This large national company was on our "do not accept" list. The agency had not stayed current with payment and knew the station was not happy but figured the rep firm would strong-arm the station into taking the business.

One of the rep firm's executives called me to complain about our policy and our GM. I stuck up for the GM who was doing exactly what he should have, and told the rep to tell the agency to clear up the delinquency and send us our money, and then we'd be happy to take the order. Rep firm and agency, sticking together, were incensed. "How can you be so bold as to demand payment before accepting this business?" they cried. "This will jeopardize all future orders," they threatened. The client—the advertiser and person actually paying the bills—knew nothing about any of this.

I decided to take action and call the client. I didn't know the BOSS, and had no personal history of doing business with the company.

Getting the name of the CEO is easy, and gets easier every day with all the information a click away. I dialed the business's main number and within seconds was talking with the executive assistant of the CEO. I explained the situation and the assistant said she'd call me back. And she did, within thirty minutes. The CEO's assistant asked that I immediately send the unpaid invoices directly to her. That was easy. Our business manager had all the details readily available since the station had been working for weeks on clearing up this account. That afternoon, the CEO's assistant called me again. She was apologetic that our payments had been so long in coming. The assistant explained to me that they, the client, had paid the agency long ago and said this delay was inexcusable and the client was not happy with—and this is the important line—not happy with "that firm we use." She didn't even refer to them by name. I was assured a check for the full amount would be prepared in the next few hours and sent out the following morning for overnight delivery. This was a Thursday afternoon. She asked if she were to send it overnight, if the station would have someone available to accept Saturday delivery, and would I give the OK to begin the commercials Monday. I did. The payment arrived and we all lived happily ever after.

Oh, not everybody. The word got back to the agency that I had made this call and the agency went ballistic, scolding the rep firm. The agency certainly couldn't defend itself with the client, and the agency never called me. They took out all their hostility on the poor rep. The entire rep office was left in such condition I understand the Walgreen's down the street was sold out of Depends that morning.

Remember the most important part of the story: that the client, the BOSS, referred to this Big Agency . . . as that "firm we use."

The agency is not to be feared and can never be permitted to stand in the way of seeing the BOSS.

$$\lambda$$

There is always the "you never know until you try" method. This story dates back more than twenty years, but it stimulates me to this day. The KMJQ sales staff had just come out of our daily sales meeting. It was just after 8:30 a.m., and I looked at my to-do list. I had told myself I wanted a face-to-face with the BOSS of one of our local supermarket chains in Houston, Fiesta Markets. His name and number were in my Day-Timer for that morning. Not thinking too much, assuming it would take me months and many attempts to actually talk with the BOSS, I casually dialed the main store's number. An operator answered, and I asked to be put through to the executive offices. I was prepared for an assistant to pick up and grill me. Imagine my shock when the next thing I heard was "Hello, Don Bonham." Yes the CEO, the BOSS. I quickly recovered, expressed my purpose, and we set a date to meet the following week. Who knows until you try?

$$\lambda$$

There is no substitute for spending time with the BOSS. When an agency buys a $4 million, 30-second commercial in the Super Bowl, where does that order come from? The agency? The marketing department? It's the BOSS talking. Anything of any significance is decided by the BOSS.

As I said, the BOSS is a person, too. Decisions often become emotional, proven by what recently took place in Indianapolis. The NFL Indianapolis Colts qualified for the playoffs with the opportunity to host the first round game. The league rule says all tickets must be sold two days prior to the game, or the game will not be televised locally. As the deadline approached, the stadium was not sold out, and Indianapolis was on the verge of a TV blackout. To the rescue came Meijer. The supermarket group, based in Michigan, is always fighting hard against the hometown, Indianapolis-headquartered, Marsh chain. Meijer purchased 1,200 tickets at an average ticket price of $100 to sell out the game and then donated all the tickets to military families. A win-win-win-win-win all around. The TV viewers were happy, the TV stations were happy, the Colts were happy, and the NFL avoided having to enforce an unpopular rule. And Meijer got a big victory on Marsh's home turf—an emotional, conceptual move proudly announced to the Indianapolis community by Doug Meijer himself. Was the $120,000 investment decided at the ad department level? This is a chairman/CEO decision, and this is the only person capable of understanding and feeling the benefit of such a move. And from what budget might the $120,000 have come?

A good way for radio stations and salespeople to begin making an effort to reach the BOSS level is with the station's existing clients. Look at all the advertisers on the station today. In how many cases does the station know the BOSS? Radio stations do $17 billion in business with thousands of clients. These businesses receive and pay invoices from radio stations. Isn't it likely the BOSSES of these businesses would take ten minutes to meet station management? Most often, the BOSS will be gracious and truly interested in taking a meeting. The meeting may be ten minutes, or sometimes two hours, and some BOSSES will be seen several times a year. And when one BOSS is met, it's like meeting three BOSSES. Because BOSSES see each other all the time, and they tell each other about people they've met.

⅄

Picture this. The conference room lights come up as the audio/visual equipment is turned off. The agency team has just concluded a primarily television-all video presentation. The room is quiet and the BOSS begins, "This is all great, terrific, but where is the radio campaign?"

Only in my dreams? Could this happen in real life? How?

I am not going to delve into the hundreds of tactics that when implemented could take radio in the direction of causing the BOSS to ask. Instead, I'll keep it simple and use just one word: prominence.

How does radio become prominent in the mind of the BOSS? So prominent that the BOSS would stop an agency presentation and ask, "Where's radio?"

Getting the BOSS to think about radio is not too hard when remembering the BOSS is a person, too. The BOSS drives around town, consumes media, hears things from a spouse, family, and friends. The BOSS is exposed to advertising. When radio stations advertise, the BOSS sees it, feels it, knows it.

The radio station consolidation of the late 1990s, and the oligopoly structure that ensued, led to the attitude of "we don't have to advertise anymore." Result? Radio recedes into the background. At the same time satellite, online, and new technology becomes . . . what? Prominent. How about those hip outdoor displays of the silhouette dancing while wearing ear buds? And the gas for $1.98 a gallon promotion that TNT ran for the premier episode of *Dallas*? Yes, a good old-fashioned radio-style promotion for a cable show backed with a full-page ad in the Sunday *New York Times*. Think the BOSS saw or heard about that?

Not that long ago, when radio stations would compete and use outside media like outdoor and television to attract attention and recruit potential listeners, the BOSS would know it.

Promotion, marketing, and advertising the radio station to the listener carries the side benefit of reaching the BOSS. A well-orchestrated, consistent investment in marketing and promotion will foster prominence. And herein lies the rub. To achieve prominence, radio must invest. There is not a gimmick or a gadget that can create prominence in a meaningful and lasting way.

Along with slashing marketing, advertising, and promotion, radio is moving more and more to network programming, eliminating local shows and feeding affiliates from New York, LA, and Nashville. These are quality shows with terrific talent. But will these stars come to meet the hometown car dealer? Show up at the state championship game? Emcee the Halloween Parade? Will running network shows improve prominence? Or is this just another economic efficiency play? Is this a path back to the 1940s? Does radio wish to recede seventy years while competing media are emerging? While TV stations continue to add local programs and personalities?

Concerts, festivals, event marketing . . . all fantastic, all attract listeners and revenue, too. Should radio be doing these? Sure, but do they produce lasting and meaningful prominence?

Radio is in a tough spot. This is not the 1960s when the high-profile radio stations were owned by large companies or well-endowed families. The question often posed is, "Are radio companies today too big?" The problem is that radio companies are not big enough. The companies who own stations are not big enough. I do not mean the radio companies should grow in the number of stations owned. That would only load the owners with more debt, solve absolutely nothing, and make things worse. What I am getting at is the ownership is weak, burdened with debt, too small, too undercapitalized to do the things necessary for radio stations to attain prominence.

Inventing new programming concepts, grooming talent, and initiating effective marketing and advertising takes brains, guts, inspiration, and hard work. It also takes money.

⚔

There once was a magazine, *BusinessWeek*. It began in 1929 and published for eighty years. It is now *Bloomberg Businessweek*. In 2009, Bloomberg bought *BusinessWeek* for $5 million, along with assuming the annual losses of $60 million.

Taking on the expense of fixing the magazine and funding the losses took a special buyer. Bloomberg, with annual profits of $2.7 billion, was such a buyer, a buyer with the depth to reinvent the product and turn the business around. Witness similar events with Warren Buffet's investments in local newspapers and Jeff Bezos buying the *Washington Post*.

Is it conceivable radio can attract this type of substantial investor and be awakened from its steady-as-she-goes operating status quo and emerge as a prominent medium in its local communities as well as in the advertising capitols of the nation?

One thing radio can't do is rest on the tired cliché's like "Well, where do you turn when there's a tornado?" Radio can remain a vital source of news, information, and caring during times of natural disasters. While this is meaningful, it is not lasting. Does radio want to be a victim of the CNN syndrome? When there is a Gulf War, CNN gets ratings.

Otherwise, there are more adult viewers on the Cartoon Network.

Even when the intent is to sound positive, I hear "radio's not going away" or "radio's not dead." Far from a bold rallying cry.

When I first set out in radio forty years ago, I read *Broadcasting* every week. The magazine was thick. *Broadcasting* covered everything back then: station transactions, radio and television programming, legislative news, interviews with entertainers and industry leaders, as well as a classified section that ran several pages.

Each week contained a full-page ad for Cox Broadcasting. The ad would feature one of the company's radio or television stations and describe something about the station's programming or an event the station just held. One week the ad would be about an anchorman in Atlanta, the next week a fundraiser in Dayton, and after that, a ratings success story from Miami. Of course, the message was very positive and every ad concluded with the following positioning line:

We Put in a Lot So You Get Out a Lot

Cox Broadcasting

Today, thousands upon thousands of radio people at stations all over the country are "putting in a lot" every day: programming, selling, working to make sure the stations run right, and making the stations a source of community pride.

No, radio is not dead. Radio is not going away.

But radio is on a plateau. And this is a dangerous place to reside.

For radio to have a future there must be investment, the fuel necessary to attack the four major issues.

In programming:

- Fresh content to attract a new generation of listeners, the 95 million millennials.
- Promotion and advertising to achieve prominence.

In sales:

- Severe reduction and limits to inventory. Not a gimmick, smart business.
- Contact with the BOSS.

CHAPTER 50

SIGNING OFF

The question comes up in every business article and self-help book, "Are you a manager or are you a leader?" I'll answer that question with a question, "Where are you?"

When the answer is "in the office," it's management. When the answer is "out in the field," it's leadership.

It's why I chose to be out on the road forty-four weeks a year. I knew I wouldn't have a clue what was really going on unless I got into the markets and spent time riding with the salespeople.

I knew some salespeople didn't look forward to this. I remember as a salesperson when one of my managers told me they were going on calls with me, it made me uncomfortable. Well guess what? No one can grow, no one can get better while in a comfort zone. Being uncomfortable is what improvement is all about.

Bill Parke stopped me in the hall one morning at WIFI-92 and asked what I was doing. "Big appointment coming up at 9:30," I boasted. "Oh yeah, where?" Bill asked. "Pep Boys. Big opportunity and I'm seeing the top guy." (Actually, I did have an appointment with the vice president of advertising, who was high up, but not Manny, Moe, or Jack.) Bill said, "Great. I'll go with you. I'll drive. Let me get my coat and keys."

So we went on the call. Bill sat there while I stumbled through my presentation, and when we got back in the car he critiqued everything I did. Was it awful for me that day? Sure it was. Did it make me a better salesman? Sure it did. I hated it that morning, but today I appreciate that my general manager took the time to make me improve.

Then there's the argument that great sales performers deserve more latitude, more freedom, don't need a manager along on calls. This is valid. But be serious. When a manager goes out with a ten-year veteran as opposed to a rookie, the manager is going to behave differently. With the veteran, the manager is going as a colleague or a coach. With the rookie, the manager goes as a trainer.

There is no activity that makes more positive impact on a station's revenue than leaders accompanying the salespeople. It is the only way to get a true read for market conditions and client wants.

A manager's role varies from call to call. At times, the manager may lead the presentation. Other times be the sidekick. Sometimes just be an observer. Management simply attending will impress the client and move the sales process along.

A good manager reads the room and knows what to do. The textbook says, "Don't jump in. That's no good. The salesperson won't learn from that." As usual, I'm not too high on textbooks. Leaders make decisions about what to do on a call based on experience and the mood of the moment. Sometimes the manager will save the day and other times watch a call go down in flames—and sometimes do something that blows the deal.

Yes, there is always a chance the manager will blow the deal. I was with one of the salespeople at a car store and the dealer was misbehaving, saying silly things just to throw us off track. I lost my patience, stood up, and said, "We're done. We're not wasting any more time here." The dealer finally stopped blabbing and sat in stunned silence as the salesperson and I walked out. "Let him stew awhile," I told her. The next day our salesperson went back and got an order. Maybe the stunt worked. Who knows?

Salespeople who are out all day making calls grow deaf to managers who sit inside all day and then lecture on how things should be done. When a manager gets out with the salesperson, the manager leads by example (although I don't advise using the stand-up-and-walk-out routine too often). Being out on calls, the salesperson sees a manager allowing themselves to be put in a vulnerable position.

This makes the manager relatable and raises the salesperson's self-esteem, too. It makes the salesperson feel better. When the going gets tough (as it does many days), most people internalize and feel isolated, lonely, and become despondent, making it very hard to perform and excite prospects. When leaders exhibit the courage to face the unknown, face the possibility of rejection, this confidence transfers to the salesperson and lightens the mood, lending itself to creativity and the magic called "sales."

⊁

Respect. Admiration. The only two words I have to describe what I think of anyone who is a true sales professional. One who puts themselves on the line every day. One who takes the risks. One with the guts and determination to persevere through the stumbling blocks, obstructions, and complications on the way to getting the order.

The $17 billion dollars in annual radio revenue may be low, it may be high, it may grow in the coming years, or it might not, but one thing is certain: what is essential to each dollar is the advertiser, and radio's connection to that customer is the salesperson.

A leader spending time on the road with salespeople shows the salesperson they are appreciated, making them feel important as people, not just employees. That time in between calls is so valuable. It is an opportunity to talk with the salesperson about their career, their life, their dreams, their future.

And what about the future? What will it be?

The future, as always, will be a by-product of how well we satisfy the wants of our customers TODAY!

And after forty years and forty thousand sales calls how do I feel?

Thankful for all that I have learned . . . so far.

The next forty thousand calls should really be something.

I'll see you on the street.

Special Thanks

I t is time to say thank you to those who made this book and my life possible.
Without whom the forty years and forty thousand sales calls would never have
been the same.

Karen
My wife of thirty-eight years, my best friend for forty-three. We were together
every step of the way. Karen always understood me, inspired me, and knew when
to tell me to cool it and give it a rest. Convincing Karen to marry me was my
greatest sale, and I cherish every moment we have together.

Geoffrey and Stephanie
Our son and daughter are a constant source of stimulation. I always strove to
make them proud and tried hard to be a good example. Geoffrey and Stephanie
were fun to be with as kids, and now as adults are even more fun. I love seeing
the man and woman each has become.

Bettina and Miles
The newest additions to our family. Our lovely daughter-in-law, Bettina, and our
grandson, Miles, born January 26, 2014, a source of immense happiness.

Mom and Dad

My mother passed early. She was just sixty-seven. I know she loved me and loved this business, too. She never tired of talking about radio and television and music as well. We used to try to tease her about being a Frank Sinatra groupie when she was a teenage bobbysoxer. I say *try* because she showed no embarrassment about it. "He was terrific," she would say, with a big wide smile. Mom had that special blend of warmth and toughness. She was mild and soft on the outside but firm in the principles, the morals, and work ethic she instilled in us growing up.

My father passed away just eight years ago. As I sat at his bedside on the night he died, I thanked him. I thanked him for always supporting me in anything I wanted to do. What more can a son ask? What more can a father do for his children? When I say support, I don't mean financially. He supported his family in that sense, but he never sent me money to buy things or go into business, nothing like that. He never made calls for me or used any of his contacts in the business to open doors. He knew I didn't want that, and he let me know I didn't need that. So in his own way, he made me stronger. I always felt him cheering me on, rooting for me, showing excitement when I'd go off on some new adventure.

I so enjoyed talking with him about media. Into his eighties, he never lost that instinct, that grasp of what was connecting with the audience. He watched every late night show on TV. He'd record them all and watch them the next morning. He'd listen to talk radio all afternoon, and in the evening look in on a new sitcom or *CSI*, or *American Idol* (he said it reminded him of *TV Teen Time*).

The day Dad died, the current morning man at WHP in Harrisburg, R.J. Harris, thoughtfully called. I was happy to spend a few minutes on the air with him reminiscing. R.J. said, although it had been nearly twenty-five years since Dad retired, a week wouldn't go by without someone in the community asking, "How's Ron Drake doing?"

My In-laws; Millie and Sanford Marateck

Karen's parents, besides giving me their daughter, provided years of encouragement and strength.

Croy Pitzer
At WMAJ in State College, PA, Croy put me on the air while I was still an undergrad at Penn State. Above that, he showed me how to work with air talent and how to make an air check session productive, techniques I use to this day.

John Tenaglia, Bill Parke, Frank Tenore
My leaders at WIFI-92. They pushed me into the deep end, to see if I could swim, and turned me into a salesman instead of an account executive.

Bob Duffy
President of Christal, leader by example.
Bob made me and my peers feel appreciated. I learned it's that feeling that makes salespeople want to perform. We remain in friendly contact, and I think about Bob and all he taught me every day.

Kevin Sweeney
I wrote about Kevin extensively in the story, but he deserves another thank you because he was so generous with the time he gave me. I will always remember the day while visiting California that he played host to my wife and children while I was off on some sales call.

Barry Baker
Somehow BB was always there . . . to bring Keymarket into River City, to take River City into Sinclair, and then at Boston Ventures to help me launch Backyard Broadcasting. Barry Baker's insight, counsel, and support have always been welcome and appreciated. And his sense of humor made every day lively.

David Smith
Chairman of Sinclair Broadcast Group. David gave me the opportunity to play a key role in the television business. Not anything I ever planned or anticipated, but it paid off tremendously for me, adding a new dimension to my career.

Copey Coppedge and Boston Ventures
Copey, Barbara Ginader, Neil Wallack, Joe Casey, and Justin Harrison, the people who stood behind Backyard Broadcasting. This is a first-class lineup of people with whom anyone would be proud to have been a partner.

Robin Smith
Robin and I have been working side by side since 1996, and the benefit was all mine. Robin's intelligence, work ethic, honesty, and practicality helped me always see choices clearly and the right paths to take.

Kerby Confer
Kerby and I met in 1975. I am happy to say we remain good friends. I always felt Kerby and I had an ideal partnership. Not because we saw eye to eye on everything, and not because we always wanted to do the same things in the same way, but because we were clear about our self-interests. Kerby and I worked to help each other get what each of us wanted. Is there a better definition of a good partnership?

And finally, the clients and prospects
A special thank you to the thousands who over the last forty years took my calls and opened the doors of your offices, shops, and showrooms to give me your time and to share your feelings and thoughts. It is from these forty thousand experiences that I have formed the opinions expressed in this book. You deserve credit as the true authors of this work.

CPSIA information can be obtained
at www.ICGtesting.com
Printed in the USA
LVOW05s2355050117
519960LV00012B/94/P